Evaluating Japan's New Grand Strategy

Robert Ward

'Robert Ward's insightful book offers profound insights into the logic and principles underpinning Japan's grand strategy, providing a roadmap to stability in today's complex and rapidly changing international environment. This essential read compellingly describes Japan's strategic evolution from the Yoshida Doctrine to Abe Shinzo's transformative approach and beyond, signifying its transition from a post-war strategy focused on stability and strong US relations to playing a more autonomous and proactive role on the world stage. As the book illustrates, Japan's increased participation in global affairs could serve as a beacon of stability amid the uncertainties in US–Japan relations and the waning of US leadership in an era marked by turbulence under the second Trump administration.

Ward explores Japan's dynamic engagement and swift advances in previously uncharted territories such as defence strategy and diplomacy, and cyber and space technologies. The book also examines Japan's leadership in economic security, highlighting its strategic efforts to reinforce supply chains and assert itself as a geo-economic power through initiatives like the CPTPP and strategic industrial policies.'

Suzuki Kazuto, Professor of Science and Technology Policy, Graduate School of Public Policy, University of Tokyo

Evaluating Japan's New Grand Strategy

Robert Ward

IISS The International Institute for Strategic Studies

The International Institute for Strategic Studies

Arundel House | 6 Temple Place | London | WC2R 2PG | UK

First published May 2025 by **Routledge**
4 Park Square, Milton Park, Abingdon, Oxon, OX14 4RN

for **The International Institute for Strategic Studies**
Arundel House, 6 Temple Place, London, WC2R 2PG, UK
www.iiss.org

Simultaneously published in the USA and Canada by **Routledge**
52 Vanderbilt Avenue, New York, NY 10017

Routledge is an imprint of Taylor & Francis, an Informa Business

© 2025 The International Institute for Strategic Studies

DIRECTOR-GENERAL AND CHIEF EXECUTIVE Dr Bastian Giegerich
SERIES EDITOR Dr Benjamin Rhode
ASSOCIATE EDITOR Alice Aveson
EDITORIAL Christopher Harder, Jill Lally, Michael Marsden, Adam Walters, Nicholas Woodroof
RESEARCH SUPPORT Ishimaru Jumpei, Kamisuna Takahiro, Kurihara Yuki, Rupert Schulenburg
PRODUCTION Alessandra Beluffi, Ravi Gopar, Jade Panganiban, James Parker, Kelly Verity
COVER ARTWORK Konishi Takuya (小西晫也), Director of Urushi Museum, Nikko, Japan and Alessandra Beluffi. Calligraphy on the front cover created by Konishi Takuya.

The International Institute for Strategic Studies is an independent centre for research, information and debate on the problems of conflict, however caused, that have, or potentially have, an important military content. The Council and Staff of the Institute are international and its membership is drawn from almost 100 countries. The Institute is independent and it alone decides what activities to conduct. It owes no allegiance to any government, any group of governments or any political or other organisation. The IISS stresses rigorous research with a forward-looking policy orientation and places particular emphasis on bringing new perspectives to the strategic debate.

The Institute's publications are designed to meet the needs of a wider audience than its own membership and are available on subscription, by mail order and in good bookshops. Further details at www.iiss.org.

British Library Cataloguing in Publication Data
A catalogue record for this book is available from the British Library

Library of Congress Cataloging in Publication Data

ADELPHI series
ISSN 1944-5571

ADELPHI AP516
ISBN 978-1-041-10132-1 / eB 978-1-003-65351-6

Contents

AUTHOR

Robert Ward is the IISS Japan Chair, carrying out independent research and writing extensively on strategic issues related to Japan, including its contemporary security and foreign policies. He is also Director of Geo-economics and Strategy and leads the Institute's work on a range of issues including global economic governance, rules and standards setting, and how economic coercion impacts policy at a national and corporate level. Prior to joining the IISS, he was editorial director at the Economist Intelligence Unit (EIU). In this capacity, he led the EIU's country and industry analysis and forecasting teams. He was also a member of the EIU's executive committee. He lived and worked in Japan from 1989 to 1996, latterly holding a position in Japan's largest credit-rating agency, the Japan Bond Research Institute. He holds bachelor's and master's degrees from Cambridge University.

ACKNOWLEDGEMENTS

This book would not have been possible but for the generous endowment of 2019 from the Government of Japan to establish the IISS Japan Chair Programme.

In writing this book, I was privileged to be able to draw on the expertise and advice of a wide range of experts and practitioners both inside and outside the Institute. In the case of the latter, these include all those who generously gave up their time to share their views on our podcast series, Japan Memo, at our webinars and during in-person meetings. I have cited some of these directly in the book, but all have enriched my understanding of often fiendishly complicated strategic issues. I would also like to thank my dear friend of nearly three decades, Robert Madsen, who helped in particular with my attempt to place Japan in the US–China–Russia great-power triangle.

In the case of the former, I would like to thank Benjamin Rhode, Editor of the *Adelphi* series, both for letting me pursue this idea and for taking his editorial scalpel to the first draft to sharpen the book's focus. Similarly, I owe Bill Emmott, Chairman of the IISS Trustees, and Mark Fitzpatrick, an IISS Associate Fellow and former Executive Director of IISS–Americas, thanks for their excellent pointers at the peer-review stage. Aspiring IISS *Adelphi* authors must also subject themselves to rigorous intellectual debate at pre-writing 'struggle sessions', at which the would-be author's ideas are challenged and improved. Here, I am grateful for their input to my IISS colleagues, who were so generous with their time and ideas: Dana Allin, Bastian Giegerich, Bill Emmott, Nigel Gould-Davies, Irene Mia, Meia Nouwens and, of course, Ben Rhode.

I also owe a considerable debt of gratitude to Alice Aveson, who, along with the copy-editing team and under a tight deadline, worked so hard to catch errors and tidy up my English. A call-out too for Alessandra Beluffi, one of the Institute's excellent team of designers, whose attention to detail on the maps will, I hope, help to support understanding of the geographic challenges of Japan's strategic position.

My thanks also to the members of the IISS Japan Chair team. Konishi Mina, based in Japan, has been tireless in her support for our work and, indeed, for that of the Institute more broadly. I am also especially grateful to Mina for persuading her father, Konishi Takuya, to create the beautiful calligraphy for the cover of the book. Thanks, too, to the members of the IISS Japan Chair team in London – Ishimaru Jumpei, Kurihara Yuki and Kamisuna Takahiro – who have been contributing to the work of the Japan Chair and whose eagle eyes were invaluable for spotting my mistakes in the transliteration of the Japanese sources.

Map 1: **Japan**

Source: IISS

©IISS

Map 2: **Japan and East Asia**

©IISS

INTRODUCTION

Japan's security environment is as severe and complex as it has ever been since the end of World War II.[1]

**Japan, Cabinet Secretariat,
'National Security Strategy of Japan', December 2022**

A grand-strategic watershed

Japan is implementing profound changes to its grand strategy – that is, to its strategy for making itself secure against threats from an increasingly unstable external environment.[2] Given that Japan is the only country to have constitutionally renounced war as the 'sovereign right of the nation' as well as the possession of 'war potential', or the means with which to fight wars, this transformation from *de jure* pacifism to a more robust defence posture is remarkable and probably unique.[3] For much of the post-Second World War period, Japan's defence policy was underpinned by the so-called Yoshida Doctrine. The term was coined in the 1970s to describe the policy of Yoshida Shigeru, Japan's pivotal prime minister in 1946–47 and 1948–54, a period of political turbulence in Japan as it adjusted to defeat and occupation.[4] Essentially a compromise between those on Japan's political right, who wanted more autonomy in defence within the parameters of Japan's security alliance with the United States, and those on the political left who opposed this alliance, and brokered by Yoshida, the doctrine held that Japan should rely on the US for its defence, keep a 'low posture' in international affairs and focus on economic growth at home.[5] Yoshida was not opposed to Japan's rearmament per se, but believed that the government's priority should be internal affairs for the immediate future and that Japan's defence plans should be commensurate with its national strength.[6] The approach to this framework was and remained pragmatic rather than dogmatic. Hence, the Japanese government's creation of the Self-Defense Forces (SDF, Japan's de facto armed forces) in 1954. The government argued that while 'war potential' was proscribed under the constitution, national self-defence was not.[7] This view was confirmed by the Cabinet Legislation Bureau, which has de facto authority over constitutional interpretation.

Underpinning the Japanese assumption of US defence cover was the US–Japan Security Treaty, which took effect in 1952, broadly at the same time as the Treaty of Peace with the Allied Powers (known as the Treaty of San Francisco), which marked the formal end of the Second World War in Asia, the end of the US-led Allied occupation and the return of Japanese sovereignty.[8] The terms of the alliance were revised amid large-scale anti-treaty demonstrations in Japan in 1960 to reflect Japanese concerns about the lack of reciprocity of the original version, which allowed the US to keep military bases in Japan, but without an obligation to defend Japan. The revised document, the Treaty of Mutual Cooperation and Security, which was renewed indefinitely in 1970, is unusual in that it does not oblige Japan to defend the US if the latter's homeland comes under attack. As such it 'compares poorly' with the reciprocity of NATO or, say, the US–Philippines Mutual Defense Treaty.[9] Zbigniew Brzezinski, national security advisor to US president Jimmy Carter in 1977–81, called Japan a 'security protectorate'.[10] Adherents to the Yoshida Doctrine had no problem with this.

Since 1955, when the long-ruling Liberal Democratic Party (LDP) was formed, the Yoshida Doctrine consensus has been challenged by three Japanese prime ministers, each of whom enjoyed exceptional political longevity by the standards of their post-war peers: Nakasone Yasuhiro in his 1982–87 premiership; Koizumi Junichiro in his 2001–06 premiership; and Abe Shinzo in his second administration in 2012–20. Notably, each of these prime ministers sought greater agency for Japan in the security alliance with the US, thus moving Japan from 'protectorate' to partner, as part of what Nakasone saw as the resolution of outstanding issues from the end of the Second World War (*sengo seiji no sōkessan*).[11]

Each also used opportunities provided by changes in the international environment to align Japan more closely with the US to force defence-policy change within Japan. Nakasone harnessed US demands – triggered by the end of US–Soviet detente in the late 1970s and early 1980s – for US allies to shoulder greater responsibility for military spending in order to break what had become a post-war domestic taboo on discussing Japan's defence needs. Koizumi used president George W. Bush's 'war on terror' after the 11 September 2001 attacks on the US to push through legislation to deploy the SDF outside Japan for the first time since 1945, albeit with caveats.

Abe, meanwhile, used lessons from the failure of his first administration in 2006–07 and rising concerns in Japan at China's coercive behaviour to bring about a raft of institutional and legal changes to Japanese security. These concerns rose sharply after 2010 when Beijing imposed a temporary curb on exports of rare-earth elements critical for some of Japan's strategic industries against a background of rising tensions over the Senkaku/Diaoyu Islands, which Japan controls and China (and Taiwan) claim.[12] Pivotal amongst Abe's changes was the reinterpretation of the constitution in 2014, which enabled

Map 3: **Senkaku/Diaoyu Islands**

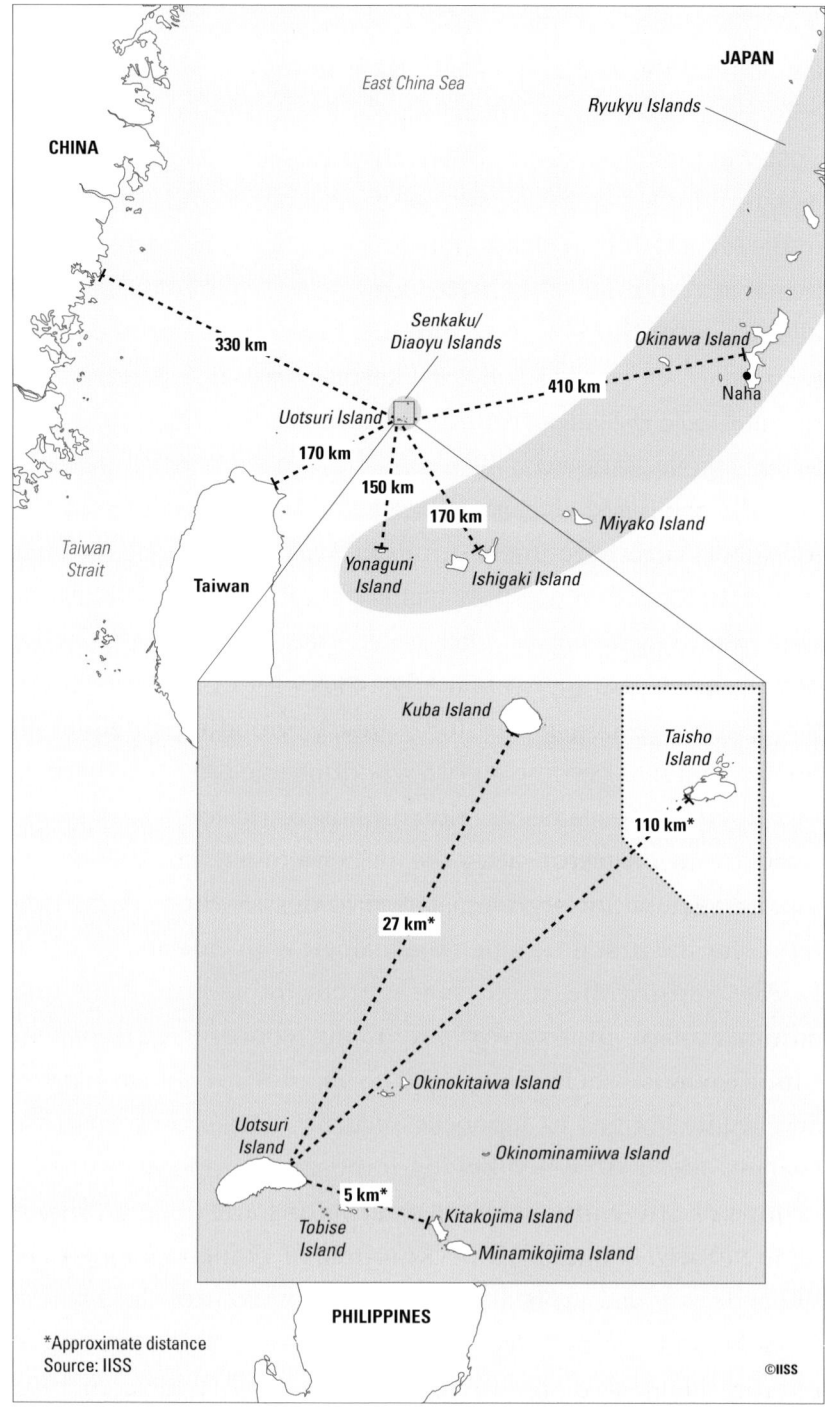

the 2015 legislation to allow the SDF to engage in collective defence for the first time. This in turn supported revisions to the Guidelines for Japan–US Defense Cooperation, the first such since 1997.[13]

But it was with the release in December 2022 of a historic new National Security Strategy (NSS) and two associated documents, the National Defense Strategy (NDS) and the Defense Buildup Program (DBP), that Japan broke with the Yoshida Doctrine.[14] These documents pointed to a sharply increased role for Japan within the US–Japan security alliance and a transformation of the dynamic of the alliance from one of 'alliance protection' to 'alliance projection into the Indo-Pacific'.[15] Not only did the new NSS posit Japan taking 'primary responsibility' for its own defence rather than relying on US guarantees under the US–Japan security treaty, but it also argued that the SDF should be able to 'disrupt and defeat invasions against its nation much earlier and at further distance' than hitherto and be capable of doing so within ten years.[16] In order to deliver on this step change in defence posture, the 2022 NSS pledged an ambitious series of reforms to boost Japanese deterrence and response capabilities, including the ability to launch counter-strikes 'against the opponent's territory', and would be funded by a sharp increase in the national defence budget to 2% of current-price GDP by fiscal year 2027–28 (April–March) from a de facto limit of just over 1% hitherto.[17] This augurs significant increases in spending that, if achieved, will take Japan's defence budget into the top five globally, up from eighth position in 2022.[18]

Japan's government has sought to reassure those concerned by the changes that they are consistent with Japan's long-held 'defence-oriented policy' and within the 'purview of Japan's Constitution'.[19] Politically, Japanese reticence in acknowledging the radical nature of the changes is not surprising.

There are lingering sensitivities in some parts of the Asia-Pacific regarding Japanese militarism and widespread atrocities committed by the Imperial Japanese military in the Second World War as well as concerns about its revival.[20] There is also opposition in some quarters within Japan to change in Japan's defence posture. Although now lacking the intensity of feeling that, say, triggered the mass demonstrations in 1960 against the revision to the US–Japan Security Treaty, which were the biggest in Japan's history, or even those of 2015 against Abe's above-noted reforms, defence policy and how it touches on the constitution remains one of Japan's few post-war domestic ideological cleavages.[21]

Yet Tokyo's claim of continuity sits uneasily with the ambition of the proposed changes. Indeed, one scholar has described Japan preparing to put itself on a 'war footing' 'as never witnessed before in the postwar period'.[22] In the DBP, for example, the Japanese Ministry of Defense (JMOD) indicates that Japan needs to 'ensure a tenacious fighting posture'.[23] Moreover, there are 43 mentions of 'warfare' in the DBP, compared with just five in the DBP's 2018 predecessor document, the Medium Term Defense Program, further illustrating the change of strategic emphasis.[24] Significant implications for Japan's defence posture also arise from the reforms, which will be discussed later in this volume, in terms of Tokyo's expanding role and increasing agency in its security alliance with the US. But a key part of this change involves a shift of emphasis from 'a functional division of labour to a geographical one', as one analyst puts it.[25] This repositions Japan away from its traditional role as the defensive 'shield' for the alliance, functioning to support the United States' role as its offensive 'spear', to a position where Japan assumes responsibility for defending itself, not least in the strategically vital Southwest Islands. This in turn allows the US to focus on the rising security challenges elsewhere in the region, particularly Taiwan. The broader direction of travel of the reforms, however, heralds deeper military integration with the US, increasing the range of support that Japan could give the US in the event of, say, a Chinese attempt to seize Taiwan by force.

The catalysts for change

China and Taiwan

There are multiple triggers for the changes in Japan's grand strategy, but the common denominator for these is the deepening security threat to Japan from China. The rapidity of the rise in China's military spending would perhaps be of concern even were China seen in Tokyo as a benign regional actor. In 2000, China's and Japan's defence budgets were roughly equivalent, but by 2020, China's was four times larger than Japan's. The gap has widened further since then (see Figure 1). But this increase has dovetailed with China's increasing threat to Taiwan's security. Beijing regards the island as a renegade province of the People's Republic of China (PRC) and, as such, as a domestic issue, and defines absorption of Taiwan as 'the core of China's core interests'.[26] If Beijing's efforts at peaceful absorption fail, it reserves the right to deploy force to achieve this goal.

The PRC's desire to absorb Taiwan dates from its founding in 1949.[27] The intensity of Beijing's efforts to 'recover' the island has ebbed and flowed since then. Despite his military rhetoric, the PRC's first leader, Mao Zedong, took a pragmatic view on Taiwan, ultimately prioritising improved relations with the US and leaving the island's return to China for later: 'we can do without Taiwan for the time being, and let it come after 100 years'.[28] Deng Xiaoping, meanwhile, preferred to concentrate on China's economic development and fostering

Figure 1: **Japanese and Chinese defence spending compared, 2000–24**

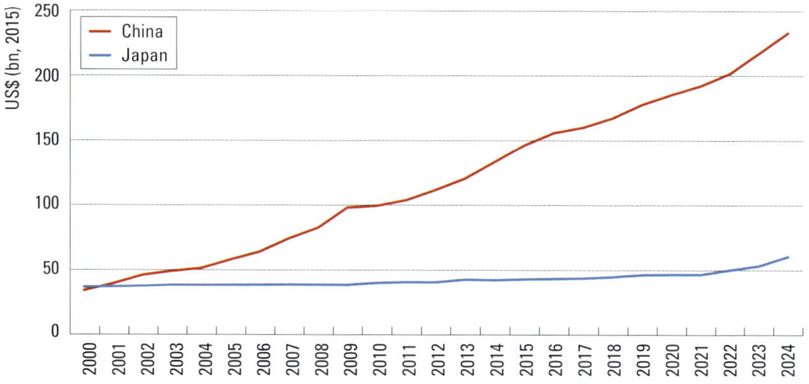

Sources: IISS, Military Balance+, milbalplus.iiss.org; IISS, *The Military Balance*, 2000–08   ©IISS

strong regional ties that would promote Chinese growth. In the 1980s, there was even a thaw in Beijing–Taipei relations, with, for example, Taiwan rejoining the Olympic Games (as Chinese Taipei) and both China and Taiwan joining the then-newish Asia-Pacific Economic Cooperation (APEC) forum in 1991.

Later in the 1990s, however, Beijing's attitude towards Taiwan hardened, reflecting international political flux after the collapse of the Soviet Union in 1991 and political changes in China, not least the rise in the importance of the People's Liberation Army (PLA) following its brutal suppression of the Tiananmen Square anti-government protests in 1989. The so-called third Taiwan Strait crisis, in 1995–96, was emblematic of this. By this time, Taiwan had made the transition to democracy under its president, Lee Teng-hui, who had studied at Kyoto Imperial University and spoke Japanese fluently, which in turn had given public opinion in Taiwan a real voice.[29] China, fearing that Taiwan was moving towards independence, tested missiles in the waters around Taiwan, and the US responded by dispatching two aircraft carriers to the vicinity of the island, in what was then the largest display of US military force in Asia since the Vietnam War. This notwithstanding, Deng's two immediate successors as leader, Jiang Zemin and Hu Jintao, both adhered broadly to Deng's priority of fostering China's economic expansion, with the hope that this would help catalyse Taiwan's absorption.[30]

Xi Jinping's formal assumption of power in 2013 signalled a switch of China's strategic priorities from his three predecessors' narrow goal of economic growth to securing and boosting China's own security and the 'great rejuvenation of the Chinese nation' to create a 'prosperous, strong, democratic, civilized, harmonious, and beautiful socialist modern country by the middle of this century'.[31] Xi includes the 'return' to China of Taiwan in this 'rejuvenation', raising concerns that he has in effect set a date by which he desires Taiwan's absorption into the PRC to be accomplished.[32] The intensification of Beijing's rhetoric regarding Taiwan and its increasing willingness to use physical intimidation against the island have significantly added to the concerns of Japan, the US and others regarding Taiwanese security. The latter was in evidence with the live-fire military drills around Taiwan after the visit to the island in 2022 by then-speaker of the US House of Representatives Nancy Pelosi and the PLA drills near Taiwan after the inauguration in 2024 of Taiwan's President Lai Ching-te, whom Beijing regards as a 'dangerous separatist'.[33]

Coercive absorption of Taiwan by China would constitute an existential threat to Japan in a number of respects. The short-term impact of a major Taiwan contingency would be catastrophic for Japan's economy. Japan's ability to supply its economy with imports depends on open sea lines of communication in both the East and South China seas. A major and prolonged conflict over Taiwan would increase risk to all shipping needing to use these seas. Japan's energy supply, always precarious given its lack of domestic resources, is particularly vulnerable: it buys 95% of its oil from the Middle East and the Japanese economy needs the equivalent of two or three 200,000 tonne tanker deliveries daily.[34] Japan's food supplies are similarly vulnerable given its reliance on food imports. Although economic-security concerns, particularly with regard to exports of high-technology items to China, as well as the deceleration of the Chinese economy suggest that Japan's economic presence in China has now peaked, China remains commercially important for Japan's growth. A major Taiwan contingency that might include US-led sanctions against China that Japan would have to join would have a severe impact on the Japanese economy.

The longer-term impact of a conquest of Taiwan by China would also be significant for Japan. Taiwan has been described as both the region's 'roundabout' and a geopolitical 'Parisian Arc de Triomphe' upon which three strategic waterways converge: the Taiwan Strait, the Bashi Channel and the Taiwan–Yonaguni channel.[35] China's absorption of Taiwan would allow Beijing to control northern access to the South China Sea, preventing the US and others from gaining access to the sea. China's allergy to freedom-of-navigation operations and view of these as a front for the US and its allies to increase their military presence in the region, coupled with Beijing's territorial disputes with a number of littoral states in Southeast Asia, suggest that this is not an unlikely scenario. Under this scenario, Japan's sea lines of communication through the South China Sea would also be subject to Chinese control, increasing Tokyo's economic vulnerability and constraining its ability to contest China's challenges to the strategic status quo in the region.

The risk to Japan in the event of a kinetic conflict between China and Taiwan is further raised by the proximity of Japanese territory to Taiwan. Taiwan lies 110 kilometres from Japan's westernmost island of Yonaguni and just 170 km from the disputed Senkaku/Diaoyu Islands. As with Taiwan, the intensity of the PRC's pressing of its claims of sovereignty over these islands has varied over the years. Since 2012, however, there has been a sharp rise in the numbers of China Coast Guard and other vessels entering the islands' territorial sea and contiguous zone.[36] The initial trigger was the nationalisation in 2012 of some of the islands by the Japanese government as it sought to head off an attempt by then Tokyo governor and leading voice in Japanese nationalist circles Ishihara Shintaro to use public funds to buy the islands in question from their private owner.[37] But since then, China's strategic focus on the Senkaku/Diaoyu should be seen as part of its broader efforts to press its territorial claims throughout the region.

China's strategy here is to 'normalise' its presence in the area, a pattern of grey-zone activity in which Beijing operates just below the level that would require a military response. This form of China's asserting of what it sees as its territorial rights is also visible in other disputed areas in the region, particularly in the South China Sea, a major throughfare for Japan's sea lines of communication. China has since supplemented this presence with a change to its own Coast Guard Law to allow it to use force against foreign vessels in waters under its 'jurisdiction', including those that it claims.[38]

Asian–European security links

The destabilisation of Japan's external environment in East Asia has been aggravated by and is increasingly interrelated with the instability in Europe caused by Russia's full-scale and brutal invasion of Ukraine in February 2022. This crystallised what the end-2022 NSS termed the 'historic changes in power balances' that directly threaten Japan.[39] Tokyo was quick to recognise the potential impact on Japan of the Russia–Ukraine conflict. In his keynote address to the IISS Shangri-La Dialogue in June 2022, Japan's then-prime minister Kishida Fumio drew attention to the links between the European and Asian security theatres in his observation that 'Ukraine today may be East Asia tomorrow'.[40] Kishida's visit to Ukrainian capital Kyiv in March 2023, the first by a Japanese prime minister to a country at war – and a European war at that – gave physical manifestation to this link.[41]

The Russia–Ukraine conflict has already had a profound impact on global geopolitics and economics. The war, which at this writing was ongoing, is the largest such in Europe since the end of the Second World War. It has also changed assumptions about future conflict, not least in its signalling of the return of 'big war' – that is, prolonged inter-state conflict at high intensity over a wide geographical area – for the first time since the 1980–88 Iran–Iraq War.[42] Russia's war against Ukraine prompted previously unthinkable innovations in economic statecraft from the G7 and a large supporting coalition of countries, both Western and non-Western. The delinking of Russia from the SWIFT international financial clearing system shortly after Russia's invasion was one example of this.[43] The agreement by the G7 in June 2024 to use frozen Russian central-bank assets to finance a loan for Ukraine was another.[44] This coalition thus imposed on Russia 'the most severe set of coercive economic measures ever inflicted against a major power in the absence of direct military hostilities between sanctioners and their target'.[45]

Japan, through its membership of the G7, was a key driver in these policy innovations. As the only Asian member of the G7, Japan also assumed an important role in making the case for continued support for Ukraine to the countries in the Global South, where the war felt strategically remote and from which many states, indeed, have been supportive of the Russian narrative. Japan's role in this regard was visible in 2023 when Japan held the presidency of the G7 and invited the leaders of non-G7 countries such as Brazil, India, Indonesia, Vietnam and others to the G7 Hiroshima Summit in June of that year.[46] Ukraine's President Volodymyr Zelenskyy was also invited.

US political scientist Robert Gilpin cited 'hegemonic struggles' as the driver of change in the international system, with such conflicts determining 'who will govern the international system and whose interests will be primarily served by the new international order'. Gilpin also observed how 'the war leads to a redistribution of territory among the states in the system, a new set of rules in the system [and] a revised international division of labour'.[47] Russia's invasion of Ukraine has the characteristics of the actions of a 'hegemonic war' in the sense of Russia as a declining power that seeks to perpetuate its claim to great-power status.[48] Indeed, the geopolitical realignments since early 2022 illustrate Gilpin's 'reordering of the basic components of the system'.[49]

One example of this is the deepening of the strategic relationship between Russia and China. Shortly ahead of the invasion, for example, China's President Xi Jinping and Russia's President Vladimir Putin described this relationship as one with 'no limits', and in 2023 Xi exhorted Putin to 'push forward these changes that have not happened for 100 years'.[50] This tightening political relationship complements the deepening Russian and Chinese military cooperation in the Indo-Pacific seen, for example, in joint aerial and naval patrols.[51] Another example is Russia's warming security relationship with North Korea since 2022, illustrated by North Korea's supplying of munitions to Russia for use against Ukraine and giving rise to fears that Russia is transferring advanced technology to North Korea.[52] In mid-2024, Putin and North Korea's leader, Kim Jong-un, concluded a mutual security pact, in effect resurrecting the Treaty of Friendship, Co-operation and Mutual Assistance that Pyongyang had concluded in 1961, but which had lapsed in 1996.

Since the Second World War ended, Japan has always been a key part of US defence strategy in Asia. Japan played important roles in providing logistics and manufacturing support for the US during the 1950–53 Korean War and in allowing the US Air Force to use airfields in Okinawa for bombing sorties during the Vietnam War. Since the Cold War, Japan has also formed the northern part of the first island chain, which runs from Japan via Taiwan, past the Philippines and down to Borneo, and in effect functions as a buffer to protect US maritime dominance in the Pacific Ocean (see Map 4). Nakasone's promise to US president Ronald Reagan in 1983 to make Japan a 'giant ship with high walls' (*ōki na kabe wo motta kyodai na fune ni shitai*), mistranslated into English by his interpreter as 'an unsinkable aircraft carrier', was one of the first public acknowledgements by a Japanese leader of Japan's military place in this strategy, notwithstanding the umbrage it caused in Japan.[53]

The Soviet Union (until the end of the 1980s), North Korea (following its first nuclear crisis of 1992–94) and China (following the third Taiwan Strait crisis of 1995–96) all constituted major security threats to Japan. But these risks were distinct and individually of a different order of magnitude from today's. Japan's relations with the Soviet Union in this period were largely dominated by the dispute over the islands to the north of Japan's northernmost island of Hokkaido, which Japan calls the Northern Territories and Russia calls the Southern Kuril Islands (see Map 5). The islands were seized by Soviet forces in late August and early September 1945 after Japan had already capitulated in the Second World War.[54] Japan's position is that the islands are occupied illegally as they were recognised as Japanese territory in the Shimoda Treaty of 1855. They were seized despite the Soviet–Japanese Neutrality Pact – a five-year non-aggression agreement that had been signed in 1941 – not having expired and Japan having finally accepted the terms

Map 4: **First island chain and Japan**

Source: IISS
©IISS

Map 5: **The Northern Territories/Southern Kuril Islands**

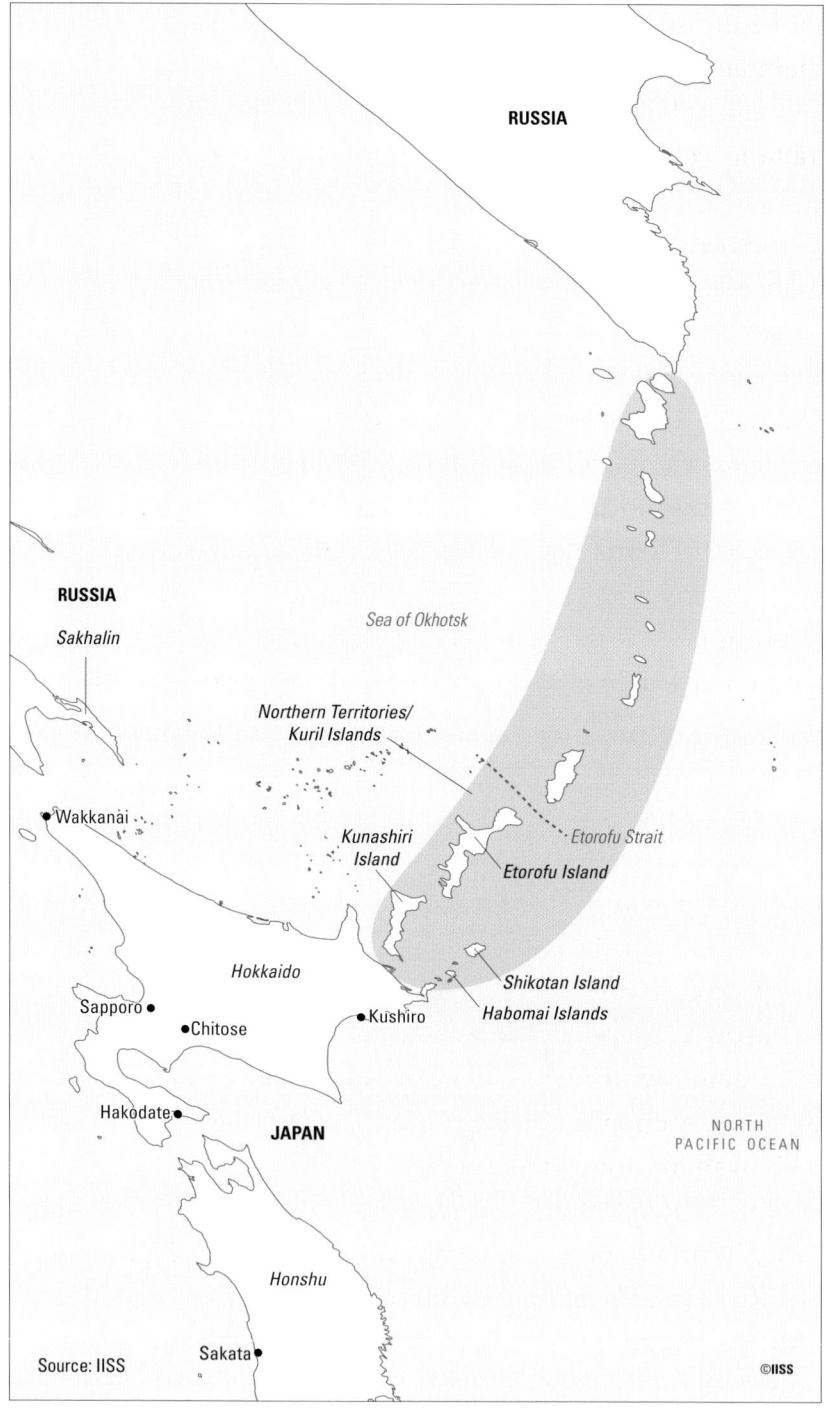

Source: IISS

©IISS

of the July 1945 Potsdam Declaration and surrendering in mid-August. The Soviet Union and subsequently Russia have maintained the position that the annexation was legal based on agreement between the US, the United Kingdom and Russia at Yalta in February 1945.[55] Japan refutes this because the treaty did not define 'the Kurils'.[56] Bilateral relations with Moscow also ebbed and flowed depending on the state of Japan's and the United States' ties with China, which were often fraught. China, meanwhile, was economically weak, having yet to embark on the period of sustained high economic growth unleashed by its joining of the World Trade Organization (WTO) in 2001. China was also at least willing to collaborate with the US and South Korea (and North Korea) in the Four-Party Talks of the late 1990s to try to defang Pyongyang's nuclear programme.

The convergence of Chinese, Russian and North Korean interests since Russia's invasion of Ukraine, in tandem with the continued expansion of Chinese military potential, Beijing's persistent menacing of Taiwan, North Korea's advancing nuclear-weapons programme and the sharp deterioration in Japan's relations with Russia since 2022, have thus driven a significant change in Japanese threat perceptions. These have been sharpened by the geographical proximity of the threats to Japanese territory, which makes Japan unique among its G7 peers. None of these has yet to experience the firing of missiles in the direction of or even over its territory, as North Korea has been doing with regard to Japan, or without warning into its exclusive economic zone (EEZ), as China did after Pelosi's visit to Taiwan in August 2022.[57]

This strategic alignment remains of concern despite Beijing, Moscow and Pyongyang being odd bedfellows. Neither China nor Russia has traditionally favoured alliances along the lines of those forged by the US, in which the US in effect shares its power in return for a strategic goal.[58] One suspects too that neither fully trusts the other. Russia, until relatively recently the more powerful of the two, surely now bridles against junior-partner status to China by virtue of its smaller and weaker economy, and China is still aggrieved at the swathe of territory lost to Russia in the nineteenth century.[59] China will also be anxious about Russia's role in North Korea, particularly if Pyongyang is able to boost the quality of its military capabilities through Russian technology transfers. Precedent suggests, too, that North Korea will remain a fickle interlocutor for both China and Russia. North Korea may have been a Sino-Soviet 'seedling' but, since the days of its founding leader Kim Il-sung, it has been successfully defying and manipulating its progenitors.[60] But the trio shares an antipathy for the world order that has been underwritten by the US, which acts as a powerful geopolitical glue.

The material danger to Japan from geopolitical realignment is aggravated by a broader threat to the status quo in the region from China's push to reorder the region in its own interests. Beijing's long-held desire to absorb Taiwan has already been noted. Beijing's territorial menacing of the Philippines, which has a maritime territorial dispute over possession of the Second Thomas Shoal (see Map 2, p. 9) with China that has grown increasingly ill-tempered, is another example of this. The reordering of the maritime space in the East and South China seas is a priority for Beijing in its objective of 'revising existing international rules and setting new rules', as one US analyst puts it.[61]

To this end, China has also been aggressively deploying 'lawfare' in pursuit of its territorial claims, prosecuted via legal extraterritoriality and deployment of its militarised coastguard and a range of other surveillance vessels.[62] Beijing's attempts at territorial coercion of Japan and others in the region move together with its desire to check the United States' presence in the region via the rejection of what it calls US 'hegemonism' and, more elliptically, as 'sabotage and coercion by outside forces' of regional interests.[63] China's criticism of US and other countries' freedom-of-navigation activities, which it sees as a tool of US power projection in its neighbourhood, is a further reflection of this desire.[64]

Testing Japanese resilience

That said, Xi's China is not a global ideological proselytiser as was that of Mao Zedong, and generates little of the quasi soft-power excitement of Maoism in its pomp.[65] Neither does Xi's Beijing have much interest in the political complexion of its national interlocutors. Rather, Beijing's relations with other countries are largely transactional. But, given China's increasing economic weight, this creates fresh challenges for Japan and others. One example can be seen in China's multibillion-US-dollar Belt and Road Initiative (BRI) global investment programme, in which countries, often those in strategically important locations for Beijing, sign up to the BRI in return for Chinese loans. China's BRI activity has sometimes been seen as exploitative, as evidenced by charges that the BRI is 'debt-trap diplomacy', and even as a means to export excess industrial capacity.[66]

Some of the problems with the BRI can be put down to China's lack of experience in large-scale international lending. That China intends to increase the quality of BRI investment indicates that Beijing recognises this.[67] But it is also indicative of Xi's worldview, which is, in the words of two observers, 'hierarchical, illiberal and coercive'.[68] In terms of hierarchy, this reflects Xi's 'tianxia' ['all under heaven'] vision of a Sino-centric world order'.[69] Glimpses of China's 'illiberal' and 'coercive' behaviour abound, whether physically in China's territorial disputes with the Philippines, Japan and others, or in the long list of its attempts at economic coercion against smaller targets, or even its abrasive 'wolf-warrior' diplomacy, which displays a contempt for accepted Western diplomatic norms.[70]

As has been described above, Japan would be one of the major geopolitical losers in a region that had fallen fully under a Chinese sphere of influence. This is not to say that China has designs on Japanese territory per se, despite recent Japanese concerns around China's intentions towards Okinawan territory, which in its former incarnation as the Ryukyu Kingdom was a tributary state of the Middle Kingdom from the fifteenth century until the 1870s when it came under Japanese control, and with the exception of the Senkaku/Diaoyu Islands. Japan's government also has concerns about Beijing's efforts to stir Okinawa's independence movement – via, for example, online influencers, some real and some not – and thus fan local discontent with the US military presence on the island, although this looks like mischief-making rather than a concerted territorial move by Beijing. But Chinese control of, say, Japan's sea lines of communication in the South and East China seas, as touched on above, would increase Japanese economic insecurity and risk constraining Japan's wider diplomatic and security room for manoeuvre, not least in its security alliance with the US.

As a result and as noted in a previous *Adelphi* volume, *Japan's Effectiveness as a Geo-economic Actor: Navigating Great-power Competition*, Japan is unlikely to acquiesce to Chinese regional hegemony.[71] This has historical echoes. Japan's relations with China have been unusual by the standards of much of the region. In 1549 it paid its last tribute mission to China, thereafter removing itself from the Chinese tribute-state system and ending its formal recognition of China's regional hegemony.[72] After the Meiji Restoration of 1868, which signalled the start of its rapid economic, institutional and military modernisation, Japan looked beyond the regional hegemon of China to the West for role models, 'inoculating' itself against the threat from the West by 'accepting the virus of modernization', in the words of the British historian J.M. Roberts.[73] China, meanwhile, took the opposite course, seeking to restore 'national spirit' and build military strength using internal resources. China's Self-Strengthening Movement, launched in 1861, was a good example of the latter.[74]

Since its total military defeat in 1945 and occupation by the US-led Allies in 1945–52, Japan has cleaved to its security alliance with the US, seeing this as the bedrock of its foreign policy, notwithstanding Tokyo's own claims of 'United-Nations centrism' (*Kokuren chūshin shugi*) in its policy.[75] Indeed, since the end of the Second World War, its policymakers have had little doubt about Japan's 'international identity' as a key member of 'the Western camp'.[76] The political dominance of the LDP, which has been a strong advocate for this 'identity', for most of the post-war period suggests broad public support for this stance. This has not always gone hand in hand with public antipathy towards China. Indeed, after Deng's successful visit to Japan in 1978, nearly 80% of those questioned for one poll indicated a favourable view of China.[77] But since the 2000s, during which anti-Japanese riots broke out in China and China opposed Japan's becoming a permanent member of the UN Security Council, opinion polls suggest that Japanese public trust in China is on a declining trend.[78] Public perceptions of the threats to Japan's national security, meanwhile, have risen, with 84% of respondents in an early 2024 poll for the *Yomiuri Shimbun* reporting either 'strongly' or 'somewhat' that Japan's security is under threat.[79] The same poll indicated that 71% of respondents supported the strengthening of Japanese defence capabilities. All this suggests that voter pressure to change Japan's international identity (i.e., as being aligned with the West) is largely absent.

Japan thus finds itself, by virtue of its desire to preserve the existing order against China's efforts to change the status quo, deepening its security alliance with the US and so putting itself on the front line of Sino-US competition. The Japanese government has been increasingly vocal about Taiwan's security. The Joint Leaders' Statement that accompanied the summit in 2021 between Japan's prime minister Suga Yoshihide and US president Joe Biden referred to 'the importance of peace and stability across the Taiwan Strait'.[80] This was the first mention of Taiwan in a US–Japan Joint Leaders' Statement since prime minister Sato Eisaku's meeting with president Richard Nixon in 1969. At that time, Sato was eager to curry favour with Nixon to further his desire to regain Japanese control from the US over Okinawa. Suga's comments were followed in May 2021 by an interview in the *Nihon Keizai Shimbun*, Japan's leading financial daily, by then-defence minister Kishi Nobuo, in which Kishi linked Taiwan's security with that of Japan.[81] Abe, at the time no longer prime minister, was even more explicit in comments he made at the end of the year to a Taiwan audience: 'A Taiwan emergency is a Japanese emergency, and therefore an emergency for the Japan–US alliance.'[82]

Since then, high-level political visits between Japan and Taiwan have also proliferated, drawing China's ire.[83] In 2023, for example, considerably more members of Japan's Diet (parliament) visited Taiwan (over 100) than did PRC legislators (fewer than ten).[84] In August 2024, ahead of the LDP leadership election that he would go on to win, Japan's prime minister at this writing, Ishiba Shigeru, also visited Taiwan along with Nakatani Gen, a former defence minister who was subsequently reappointed to the role in Ishiba's cabinet.[85] Within this context it is also worth noting Taiwan's close historical links with Japan, not least its status as a Japanese colony from 1895, when Japan acquired the island after its victory in the first Sino-Japanese war, until Japan's military defeat in 1945.

Beijing's increasing menacing of the island should be seen in the context of Xi's including of Taiwan's 'return' to Beijing in China's 'national rejuvenation', which is also linked to his goal of China achieving great-power status by mid-century, broadly the centenary of the founding of the PRC.[86] Taiwan's proximity to Japanese territory has already been noted. But this means that there is a high risk that, in the event of a full-scale attack by China on Taiwan, Japanese territory would at the very least sustain collateral damage. Japan's Nansei or Southwest Islands, which stretch from Yonaguni through Okinawa and up to the southernmost main island of Kyushu, would likely be key for Chinese anti-access/area-denial (A2/AD) strategies and any US-led response to these. The latter would include US forces based in Japan, particularly at Kadena Air Base on Okinawa, which China may then target. The focus on the Southwest Islands in the 2022 NSS, NDS and the DBP reflects Tokyo's awareness of the strategic vulnerability of this area. Given the time it would take the US to mobilise a full-scale military response to a Chinese attack on Taiwan, Japanese resilience and response lethality in the early phase of such a conflict would be critical to successfully defending Taiwan, assuming full Japanese military involvement.

'Hardware' and 'software'

This raises a number of questions that this *Adelphi* book seeks to answer. Much current analysis of Japan's shifting grand strategy focuses on why this is historic by the standards of Tokyo's post-war past. This volume considers whether the enabling reforms and efforts to boost Japanese security resilience are sufficiently robust to fulfil Tokyo's goal of ensuring its own security and regional stability, even in the scenario of a Chinese attack on Taiwan.

In doing so, this *Adelphi* also makes several assumptions, which are derived from discussions with senior Japanese policymakers. One is that maintaining Taiwan's security is the strategic focus of Japan's security reforms and in effect a pillar of Japanese grand strategy. This holds even though Japan prefers, for domestic political and foreign-policy reasons, to maintain its own strategic ambiguity about any role for it in a Taiwan contingency. (Unlike the US with its Taiwan Relations Act, Japan also has no legal provision to defend Taiwan.[87])

Another assumption is that, in the event of an unambiguous Taiwan emergency, which may include a blockade of Taiwan by China, Japan's Diet is likely to authorise measures to cooperate with the US where needed. Taiwan's security is simply too strategically important for Japan to remain inactive under such a scenario. The thresholds set for the SDF to engage in collective self-defence even if Japan is not directly itself under attack are kept broad in prime minister Abe Shinzo's 2014 reinterpretation of Article 9 of the constitution and the accompanying legislation in 2015, and allow for flexibility in interpretation.[88] But, given Taiwan's strategic value to Japan, this book assumes that an attack by China on Taiwan would constitute a threat to 'Japan's survival' and thus meet one of these conditions.[89]

Critically, this also assumes a US military response under such a scenario. This is, of course, not a given. Japan's strategic predicament lies in its dependence for its security on an ally over which it has little control. Unlike many countries in Western Europe, which enjoy a degree of collective security by virtue of their NATO membership, albeit underwritten by the US, Japan is strategically isolated in its region. Japan's grand strategy therefore needs to be directed at influencing the United States' strategic commitment to Asian security. This explains Tokyo's efforts to increase Japanese agency in and thus its value to the alliance through the above-noted defence reforms. An assessment of the effectiveness of Japanese grand strategy therefore needs to evaluate these factors as well as be stress-tested against the possibility of war.

This book also seeks to address Japanese strategic robustness and agency in the broadest sense. It does not seek to illuminate how Japan might respond to, say, a possible spectrum of grey-zone coercion against Taiwan from China that falls short of kinetic threat, or possible roles for Japan in such a scenario within its security alliance with the US – for example, whether Japan's role would be limited to defending the Japanese homeland, or whether it would take a fuller role defending US military forces. Neither does it set out to debate in depth the advantages or disadvantages of specific military equipment or SDF deployments, important though these are for Japan's ability to deter and respond.

The underlying question for this *Adelphi* of Japan's strategic resilience is also important. The regional military balance is, after all, shifting rapidly in China's favour as Beijing presses on with its military modernisation and the supporting securitisation of its economy. Thus, while the US would almost certainly take the lead in deciding whether to fight for Taiwan, Japan's response would play a vital role in determining the outcome of any fight. By extension, therefore, Japanese strategic resilience is now a critical component of the credibility of the United States' deterrence and response capabilities in the region.

Tokyo has chosen to frame its ability to shape and respond to the geopolitical shifts in its near abroad 'by taking a panoramic view of the diverse dimensions of international relations' and deploying 'comprehensive national power'.[90] Japan's government defines this power as including Japan's 'diplomatic, defense, economic, technological and intelligence capabilities'.[91] Comprehensive national power should speak to Japan's strengths, especially given its complementing geo-economic power. But, again, are Japan's strengths within this self-selected power spectrum sufficient given the scale of the challenge it faces, not just from China but also from North Korea and, since its invasion of Ukraine, Russia?

'Hardware' is one thing, but 'software' quite another. The effective wielding of national power demands an underpinning 'software' of strategic culture. British strategist and international-relations scholar Colin Gray described strategic culture as a 'rich and distilled source of influence which might "cause" behaviour', adding that one can see strategic culture as 'socially constructed by both people and institutions, which proceed to behave to some degree culturally' and how this bears on 'whether, why, and how people, polities and would-be polities, fight'.[92] In *The Russian Way of Deterrence: Strategic Culture, Coercion, and War*, political scientist Dima Adamsky offers a useful definition of strategic culture as:

> a set of shared values, norms, beliefs, assumptions, and narratives (written, oral, formal and informal), which shape and sometimes determine the collective identity, instincts and modus operandi of a given strategic community in its approach to questions of peace and war (i.e., the appropriate ends, means, and ways of achieving national security objectives).[93]

Thus, strategic culture is a complex cocktail of ingredients including historical experience, the impact of geography on strategic thinking, the character of national institutions and shared assumptions by policymakers. This matters in Japan's case against the backdrop of the strong anti-militarism that has characterised Japanese strategic culture for much of the post-war period. Japan is unusual in having been demilitarised and then come under pressure to rearm shortly thereafter.

The US-led Allied occupation demilitarised Japan immediately after the Second World War with the disbanding of the Imperial Japanese forces and the breaking up of its defence-industrial base. It reversed course as the Cold War started in the late 1940s, with the US pressuring Tokyo to rearm to help ensure regional stability. Although Germany is often seen as the main comparator for Japan in terms of security, there are a number of differences, including Germany's constitutional lack of constraints on maintaining 'war potential', provided that the country's armed forces are 'for [the] purpose of defence'.[94] Few, if any, countries, therefore, have travelled the strategic distance that Japan is now attempting.

It is important to consider Japan's preparedness for conflict for three main reasons. The first is the role of Japan as a critical security ally of the US. During the Biden presidency, given the potency of the challenge to regional stability from China and others, the US shifted from the 'hub and spokes' system of bilateral alliances that prevailed in the Cold War to a networked system of allies and partners, in which these have greater agency. At the 2024 IISS Shangri-La Dialogue, then US defense secretary Lloyd Austin described this strategic shift as a 'new convergence' that would strengthen and make more resilient the United States' 'network of partnerships'.[95] Importantly, it also allows the US to amplify its increasingly stretched resources in the region. Examples of this new convergence include the Quadrilateral Security Dialogue, known as the Quad and involving Australia, India, Japan and the US, and the AUKUS information- and technology-sharing partnership between Australia, the UK and the US. Japan's active defence diplomacy has embraced this new convergence and will find itself shouldering an increasing deterrence and response burden in the region as a result.

The second reason is the unpredictability of the US. Although Japan's relations with the US were exceptionally strong during the Biden–Kishida years, concerns remain in Tokyo about the sustainability of US engagement in the region given the uncertainties of US politics on both the Democrat and Republican sides. Japan's defence resilience is important as insurance against the ebb and flow of US interest in the region. Japan's defence reforms thus have one eye on boosting US trust in Japanese capabilities and so sustaining US interest in the region. This has become particularly urgent since Donald Trump, with his more transactional approach to foreign policy, returned to the White House.[96] And the third reason for considering Japan's preparedness for conflict is the rising likelihood of conflict. In January 2024, then UK defence secretary Grant Shapps described 'moving from a post-war to a pre-war world', citing the threats from China, North Korea and Russia and others.[97] Against this background, Japan's defence-reform ambitions become even more urgent, as does an assessment as to whether its evolving grand strategy is up to the task at hand.

CHAPTER ONE

Japan's shifting strategic compass

Geography is the most fundamental factor in the foreign policy of states because it is the most permanent. Ministers come and ministers go, even dictators die, but mountain ranges stand undisturbed.[1]

Nicholas J. Spykman, *America's Strategy in World Politics: The United States and the Balance of Power*, 1942

Japan's basic philosophy of international relations [is a] belief in world interdependence.[2]

Kosaka Masataka, *Options for Japan's Foreign Policy*, Adelphi Paper 97, 1973

Maritime Japan

Japan's geography has been one of the key reasons for its unusual pattern of interaction with its region and for the successes and failures of its grand strategy. Sitting in the northwest corner of the Pacific Basin, the Japanese archipelago consists of four main islands and some 14,000 islands in total.[3] Japan's territory extends around 2,900 kilometres – or about twice the length of Italy – from its sub-arctic north next to Russia to its sub-tropical south not far from Taiwan, but the land is just 400 km or so wide at its broadest. With a land area of some 378,000 square kilometres, Japan is about the same size as Germany or Vietnam.[4] This topography, coupled with the wide distribution of outlying islands, has given Japan the sixth-largest marine territory in the world (see Map 6). The combined coastline of these outlying islands is longer than all of Brazil's coastline, but constitutes just 20% of Japan's total.[5] The sea has thus played a central role in Japanese history – as a protector against attempted Mongol

Map 6: **Japan's maritime territory**

RUSSIA

Sea of Okhotsk

Alaska (US)

RUSSIA

CHINA

Rishiri Island

NORTH KOREA

Sea of Japan (East Sea)

Tsushima Island

SOUTH KOREA

■ Tokyo

East China Sea

CHINA

JAPAN

Ryukyu Islands

Senkaku/ Diaoyu Islands

Okinawa Island

Ogasawara Islands

Iwo Islands

Minamitorishima Island

Taiwan

Yonaguni Island

Okinotori Islands

PACIFIC OCEAN

PHILIPPINES

Guam (US)

Japan's territorial waters
0–12 nautical miles

Japan's exclusive economic zone (EEZ)
12–200 nautical miles

Source: IISS

©IISS

invasion in the thirteenth century; as an enabler of the near-total national seclusion of the *sakoku* (national isolation) period in the seventeenth to mid-nineteenth centuries; as a conduit for the forced opening to the world again triggered by the arrival of Commodore Matthew C. Perry's Black Ships from the United States in Edo Bay (now Tokyo Bay) in 1853; and as a means of transportation for Japan's transformation into a global export powerhouse after the Second World War.[6]

Four strategic phases

Meiji maritime realism

The Meiji Restoration of 1868 was one of the critical turning points in Japanese history. The Restoration looked in part to the past in the return of direct rule by the emperor after 600 years of *Shogun* (generalissimo) rule in the emperor's name, and was the result of a largely peaceful revolution led by anti-*shogunate* samurai radicals.[7] But, more importantly, its leaders wanted to create a new Japan that could, in the words of Sanjo Sanetomi, an influential court noble and important figure in the Restoration, 'stand equal with foreign countries'.[8] The changes it wrought societally and, eventually, in Japan's international position were revolutionary. These included the end of the 'decentralised' feudalism in Japan and the establishment of new state institutions, which transformed Japan in administrative, economic, diplomatic and military terms.[9]

One historian has called the Restoration 'the most remarkable accomplishment by any nation in modern history', ranking alongside the US and French revolutions.[10] Another has described it as a 'Japanese 1688' after the Glorious Revolution of that year, a constitutional watershed for England.[11] It is difficult to imagine that Japan would have had the resources or ambition to influence and then later to try to subjugate swathes of the Asian mainland but for the breadth of changes undertaken during the Meiji Restoration. If after the 1894–95 First Sino-Japanese War, which was fought over influence over Korea, until then a Chinese tribute state, and which Japan won, Japan was on the road to becoming itself a great power, by the early twentieth century, after its victory in the 1904–05 Russo-Japanese War, fought over rival ambitions in Korea and Manchuria, it had become one.

Japan's grand-strategic trajectory from 1868 to today can, for the purposes of this *Adelphi*, be divided broadly into four phases. During the first, which dates from the Restoration until the 1920s, Japan sought to build state power to preserve its independence in the face of Western and Russian encroachment in the region. The extrication of Japan from the West's Asian treaty-port system was a key driver of this.[12] Imposed on Japan through the 'unequal treaties' after the country's forced opening in the 1850s, the system allowed foreigners to control nearly all Japan's foreign trade, and lasted into the 1890s.[13]

During this period Japan also saw its strategic interests as lying with the world's leading maritime states and in integrating itself within the international order underwritten by them. This found expression in the Anglo-Japanese Alliance of 1902–23, the first pact of equals between a European and an Asian power, which allowed the United Kingdom and Japan to contain growing Russian influence in China and enabled London to focus its military resources on the rising German threat in Europe from the early 1900s. It was also one of the anchors of Japanese foreign policy in the period. The alliance was allowed to lapse in 1923 at US urging, reflecting, inter alia, Washington's concerns about Japan's own spreading influence in China.[14] Overall, this reflected a predominantly realistic view of Japanese national interest.

The 'continentalism' cul-de-sac

The second phase lasted from the 1920s to the end of the Second World War, and was driven by a combination of factors including domestic economic volatility, the increasing role of the Imperial armed forces in Japan's domestic politics, civil war in China and deteriorating US–Japan relations. In this period, Japanese strategy shifted from working within the existing international order underwritten by the maritime power of the British Empire and the rapidly rising US, to the building of an empire on the Asian mainland. (Japan's acquisitions of Taiwan in 1895, Manchuria in 1905 and Korea in 1910 were broadly absorbed within the order of the time, with Japan remaining alert to balances of power and the need to avoid 'Western' great-power intervention.) The purpose of this new empire was to create an exclusive Japanese sphere of influence in the region and a new continental order, the Greater East Asia Co-Prosperity Sphere, that would be economically self-sufficient and that Japan would lead.

Japan had thus strayed strategically from 'maritime nation' (*kaiyō kokka*) to 'continental nation' (*tairiku kokka*).[15] One result of this was that its diplomacy became 'purely military-oriented' and ideological rather than pragmatic.[16] Its withdrawal from the League of Nations in 1933, in protest at the League's denunciation of its occupation of Manchuria, signalled its 'rejection of the global order', triggering its diplomatic isolation and aligning it with the challenger states to the global order led by Germany and Italy.[17] The roots of Japan's catastrophic defeat in 1945 lie in the strategic dead end of this 'continentalism'. Japan's removal of itself from the global maritime order showed a profound misunderstanding of the strategic advantages conferred on it by its 'gift of geography' as an island nation and of its vulnerabilities, not least its economic dependence on the maritime domain and international law as a means of sustaining the domain's openness.[18]

Yoshida Doctrine pragmatism

The third phase, from the end of the US-led occupation in 1952 until the start of the second premiership of Abe Shinzo in 2012, saw a return of Japan's strategic identity as a member of the global order underwritten by the world's dominant maritime power, this time the US. This was underpinned by the return of a realistic and pragmatic view in Tokyo of how to obtain Japanese security, and was influenced both by the overwhelming dominance of the US and by the catastrophic nature of Japan's military defeat. As Japanese historian Iriye Akira notes, Japan's defeat in 1945 was complete, transforming it at the stroke of a pen from an Asian great power to a 'small island nation'.[19]

Under the US-led occupation Japan was demilitarised and democratised in order to prevent its 'will to war' from re-emerging and challenging the US-led post-war order.[20] A slew of reforms was implemented, including the abolition of domestic-security laws, the introduction of voting for women, the legalisation of unions, and the dissolution of the *zaibatsu* financial and industrial conglomerates. This was another revolution for Japan, its second in just under 80 years. At the time, Miyazawa Kiichi, then a bureaucrat in Japan's Ministry of Finance and later a leading figure in the Liberal Democratic Party (LDP) and prime minister in 1991–93, observed that there had been as much change in Japan in the seven years of occupation as there would have been in 100 years had events proceeded normally.[21]

The relationship between the US and Japan during the occupation was without historical precedent, both in the 'focused intensity' of the US on Japan and in the 'messianic fervour' of US General Douglas MacArthur, the Supreme Commander for the Allied Powers in Japan.[22] Unlike in occupied Germany, the administration of defeated Japan was not divided between the victorious Allies – the US, the Soviet Union, the UK and France. The extent of US control over Japan was evident in the imposing on it in 1946 of a new constitution to replace the Meiji constitution of 1889. The document, dubbed the 'MacArthur constitution' after MacArthur's leading role in creating it, has been described as an un-Japanese 'product', with 'language and concepts patched together from the Anglo-American political tradition'.[23] Notably, the new constitution 'renounce[s] war as a sovereign right' in its Article 9. While nationalists in Japan have long chafed at the loss of sovereignty this 'alien' constitution implies, it remains unchanged and now enjoys the distinction of being the world's oldest unamended such document. MacArthur regarded the constitution as the most important accomplishment of the Allied occupation.[24]

Against this background it is not surprising that Japan's post-1952 relationship with the US has been central to its foreign and security policy, with the US–Japan security alliance functioning as the anchor for its grand strategy. This will also remain the case, largely because for Japan there is no realistic alternative to the US as a security ally given the volatile geopolitical make-up of its neighbourhood and the scale of the security challenge from China. Despite Chinese concerns to the contrary, the prospect of the formation of an 'Asian NATO' is remote. In addition to the lingering historical and sovereignty issues impeding a formal alliance between Japan and South Korea, which is Japan's closest neighbour and with which it shares a number of geopolitical interests, the region is too politically, economically and culturally disparate and the distances between countries too vast for a NATO-like organisation to be viable.

No government in Tokyo since the Treaty of San Francisco returned sovereignty to Japan in 1952 has seriously sought formally to change the country's security relationship with the US.

This has held despite sometimes profound bilateral differences on defence policy. From the 1950s, for example, the US agitated for Japan to rebuild its own defence capabilities and to function as a bulwark against Soviet encroachment in East Asia as it had been against Tsarist Russia in the first decade of the century. Japan's prime ministers, meanwhile, mostly preferred to focus on the country's post-war economic recovery and development. Even during the worst of the US–Japan economic friction of the 1980s and early 1990s there was no serious questioning in Tokyo of the importance of Japan's security relationship with the US. Even pivotal post-war prime ministers such as Nakasone Yasuhiro in his 1982–87 administration, who railed at what they saw as Japan's subordinate position as the alliance's defensive 'shield', while the US held the 'spear' of offensive capabilities, saw the alliance as essential to Japanese security.

At this writing in early 2025, the LDP had ruled Japan for all but around four of the 69 years since its founding in 1955. Between 1955 and its fall from power after the 1993 general election, the LDP governed alone. From its return to power in 1994 until today – and excluding 2009–12, when it was in opposition for the second time – the LDP has ruled in coalition with much smaller parties. The party has thus played the dominant role in shaping Japanese external policy. As described in the Introduction, for much of the post-war period until recently, the LDP was dominated by intra-party factions adhering broadly to the Yoshida Doctrine – that is, by those advocating that Japan should adopt a 'low posture' internationally, or 'economics above all' foreign policy.[25] In essence, this was 'economic realism' underwritten by the US security guarantee.[26] The Yoshida Doctrine followers also de facto agreed to defer constitutional revision, one of the core policies of the LDP from its founding, notably of the document's Article 9.[27]

A pragmatic attitude to constitutional reinterpretation, which the opposition Socialist Party and Japanese Communist Party also vehemently opposed, was also a means of ensuring domestic political stability and the sustainability of the US security alliance.

The party's challenger factions, essentially conservative nationalists, under prime ministers Kishi Nobusuke (in office 1957–60), Nakasone Yasuhiro, Koizumi Junichiro (2001–06) and Abe Shinzo (2006–07 and 2012–20), who was also Kishi's grandson, sought to move Japan away from the US-imposed post-war constraints on Japanese sovereignty.[28] Breaking with the Yoshida Doctrine by rearming, increasing Japan's agency within the US security alliance and revising the constitution were key aims for each. As such, this group is seen by some as 'revisionist', which has occasionally created friction with US administrations. The most recent example of this came in the early days of Abe's second premiership. Abe's conservative and 'revisionist' views sat ill with US president Barack Obama's administration, which viewed his return to power with concern.[29]

The Abe structural break

While Nakasone had broken the post-war taboo on discussing defence issues and Koizumi had taken an opportunistic approach to using changes in Japan's external environment to advance desired changes in Japan's defence posture, it was Abe in his second term as prime minister who created a structured and maritime-centric framework for Japan's grand strategy. He was the first Japanese post-war prime minister to pursue such an integrated policy platform and in so doing ushered in the fourth phase of Japan's post-war strategic journey that was augmented by the Kishida Fumio administration's ambitious defence-reform plans.

Previous prime ministers had of course recognised the importance of the maritime domain to Japan. Yoshida Shigeru had noted in the 1950s that Japan was a maritime nation, although he saw this within the terms of what later became known as his 'Doctrine'.[30] In this, Yoshida was also drawing a line under Japan's failed 'continentalism' of the interwar period. Prime minister Ohira Masayoshi, in office in 1978–80, created the outline of a maritime-centred policy in his Pacific Basin Cooperation Concept. This recognised that technological change had 'turned the vast Pacific Ocean into an inland sea' and sought to create a 'regional community' in this maritime space.[31] Ohira died in office before progress could be made on the idea, but the Concept was an early prototype of what later became the Asia-Pacific Economic Cooperation (APEC) forum, for which Japan was, along with Australia, a key agitator.

The transformation of the security aspect of Japan's maritime posture took another step forward in 1981, when, after a summit meeting with US president Ronald Reagan in Washington, Ohira's successor as prime minister, Suzuki Zenko, indicated in a press conference that Japanese defence policy would expand to include the defence of sea lanes in an arc of up to 1,000 nautical miles from Japan.[32] The Reagan administration had been pushing for Japan to take on a greater maritime-security role.[33] But Suzuki's comments set off predictable political disquiet back in Japan, not least because of what this implied for the expanded development of Japan's military potential given the size of the area to be defended and the nature of the threat from Soviet forces.

Yet Abe's contribution to Japan's view of its strategic identity and to how it should ensure its security was to understand the link between the strengths and vulnerabilities of its geographic position and his early identification of China as a potential threat to Japan and the broader rules-based order.

Thus, at the core of Abe's strategic vision were two interrelated ideas: one to prevent Japan and Asia from falling under Chinese hegemony, and the other to increase Japanese agency within its security alliance with the US. Abe's analysis of China was prescient given that his initial articulation of these views came at a time when the US and the European Union, for example, still believed that China's integration into the global economy after its accession to the World Trade Organization (WTO) in 2001 would turn it into a cooperative international actor. One example is Abe's book and de facto political manifesto of 2006, *Utsukushii Kuni E* (Towards a beautiful country), where he devotes considerable space to China, highlighting the unequal distribution of the economic dividends from Chinese economic growth, China's antagonism towards Japan and his concerns about Sino-Taiwan relations.[34]

In 2012, immediately after taking office as prime minister for the second time, Abe wrote an article for a non-Japanese channel, Project Syndicate, in which he observed that 'peace, stability, and freedom of navigation in the Pacific Ocean are inseparable from peace, stability, and freedom of navigation in the Indian Ocean'. He described Japan as 'one of the oldest seafaring democracies in Asia', urged Japan to 'play a greater role in preserving the common good in both regions' and warned of the risk of the South China Sea becoming a 'Lake Beijing' and acting as a springboard for Chinese military action in the region.[35] Abe also wrote of the importance of the rule of law in international relations, a subject on which he expanded in his keynote address to the 13th IISS Shangri-La Dialogue in May–June 2014.[36]

In this one can detect the firming contours of Abe's Free and Open Indo-Pacific (FOIP) concept of 2016 and indeed the impetus behind his sponsorship of the Quadrilateral Security Dialogue (known as the Quad and including Australia, India,

Japan and the US). Updated by prime minister Kishida Fumio in 2024, FOIP is an explicit acknowledgement of Japan's 'belief in world interdependence' noted by Japanese international-relations scholar and strategist Kosaka Masataka in the quotation at the start of this chapter from his 1973 *Adelphi* paper. Although Kosaka was writing at a time when memories of Japan's attempts to impose economic autarky on Asia by force were still fresh, Japan's lack of formal allies apart from the US and the threats to it from its immediate neighbourhood make the concept of 'interdependence' particularly important within the Japanese context.

A triangle and triangulation

Japan's China 'obsession'

While the US has been the anchor of Japan's grand strategy since the end of the Second World War, China has, in the words of Japanese international-relations scholar Royama Michio, been a 'political obsession of the Japanese' and thus loomed large in Tokyo's security thinking.[37] This is not surprising. China, by virtue of its size, has always had an outsized political and economic impact in Asia, even during the Chinese decline and domestic turbulence of the nineteenth and early twentieth centuries. The ebb and flow of Chinese state power also influenced Japan's relations with its immediate regional interlocutors, notably Korea. The 1,500 years or so of intense cultural exchange between China and Japan have obviously also had a profound impact on Japan. US political scientist Arthur Doak Barnett calls Japan's cultural importation from China 'one of the most massive programs of cultural borrowing in history'.[38] The four-character Japanese phrase *dōbun dōshu* (common script, common race) may be less often used in contemporary Japan, but it evidences the special relationship that has long existed between the two countries.[39] This sets Sino-Japanese relations apart from those Japan has with, say, the US or with the Soviet Union/Russia.

Japan's history between the Meiji Restoration and its defeat in 1945 was dominated by two wars it fought against China. Japan won the first, obtaining Taiwan as a colony as a result, and lost the second. Japan fought the First Sino-Japanese War (1894–95) against a backdrop of the destabilisation of the Asian balance of power in the late nineteenth century that arose from the weakening of the Chinese state and fears in Tokyo that Russia rather than Japan might be the beneficiary.[40] It fought the Second Sino-Japanese War, which lasted from Japan's invasion of Manchuria in 1931 until its defeat in 1945, against a turbulent domestic and international backdrop. This included its own rising political instability in which Japan's military in effect assassinated its way to power; a crisis in global governance set off by the Great Depression, which had hit Japan particularly hard; and fears in Tokyo about Soviet expansionism in East Asia and civil war in China.[41] In the first war, Japan was clear about its strategic objectives and adhered to the international law of the time. In the second, it overreached and, with the Japanese attack on Pearl Harbor in 1941, turned the US into an implacable adversary that could challenge it over multiple new theatres. In each, therefore, Japan's policy towards China also triggered profound turning points in its own political and geopolitical trajectory.

Notwithstanding Japan's close political and security relations with the US after the Second World War, Tokyo has not always followed the US line on relations with Beijing. But Japan's strategic room for manoeuvre has waxed and waned depending on the state of Sino-US relations. Singapore's founding father Lee Kuan Yew noted the 'isosceles triangle theory', which held that 'relations between Japan, the US and China are most stable when they take the form of an isosceles triangle. This means maintaining a triangular configuration in which US–Japan ties are closer than either Sino-Japanese relations or Sino-American relations'.[42] But Japan's ability to navigate relations with its immediate continental interlocutors since the end of the Second World War has also often been influenced by the broader backdrop of how Sino-US relations have dovetailed with relations with the Soviet Union and then Russia.

In the middle of the twentieth century, prime minister Yoshida saw rebuilding Japanese commercial relations with China as an important part of restoring Japan's economic health, despite US hostility to the then newly established Communist state. Yoshida was also a 'China specialist', who had spent much of his career as a diplomat in China, believing that it was 'unthinkable' that Japan could thrive without a close relationship with China.[43] In 1951, Yoshida wrote in an article for the *Foreign Affairs* journal that 'red or white China remains our next-door neighbour', noting the importance of 'geography and economic laws' in determining the course of Sino-Japanese relations.[44] Yoshida's view that Japanese trade with China could also serve as a 'fifth column for democracy against the communists' prefigured by several decades the hopes noted above that integrating China into the world economy after its accession to the WTO in 2001 would help China democratise and stabilise international relations.[45] Despite some hurdles such as the 1958 crisis in bilateral relations (see Chapter Two), subsequent Japanese prime ministers and the Chinese government also promoted Sino-Japanese trade, with the result that by the early 1960s bilateral trade had resumed.[46] Although trade with China was a small percentage of Japan's overall trade, for China, then a much smaller economy, trade with Japan became increasingly important both economically and as a strategic offset to the collapse in its trade with the Soviet Union as Sino-Soviet relations chilled.[47] Sino-Japanese trade also rose quickly, albeit from a small base. Indeed, by 1965 Japan had become China's largest trading partner by value, overtaking the Soviet Union.[48] Key for Japan in nurturing this trade, however, was the delinking of its economic and political relations with China, so-called *seikei bunri*. This separation allowed Tokyo to build economic ties with Beijing while maintaining diplomatic ties with Taipei and thus also reassuring its US ally that it would not extend diplomatic recognition to Beijing.

Prime minister Tanaka Kakuei's move to quickly normalise political relations with China in 1972, in the wake of US president Richard Nixon's shock announcement in 1971 that he intended to do the same, partly reflected political opportunism. Tanaka's own political focus and interest was domestic, and his flagship policy was a major domestic infrastructure-building programme outlined in his book and de facto political manifesto, *Nihon Rettō Kaizō Ron* (Plan to remodel the Japanese archipelago), which was published in June 1972, was a best-seller at the time and remains in print to this day. But in order to secure sufficient votes in the LDP leadership contest, Tanaka had secured the support of key LDP faction leader Miki Takeo, who was a champion of closer relations with Beijing.[49] Miki desired the normalisation of bilateral relations and conclusion of a peace treaty with China as the price for the support of his faction for Tanaka's candidacy.[50] For Tanaka, rapprochement with Beijing was also an opportunity for the LDP to neutralise Communist China as a source of the often-bitter ideological divisions that had riven Japan since the founding of the People's Republic of China (PRC).[51] Tanaka was elected prime minister in July 1972 and went to Beijing in September of the same year, just seven months after Nixon's historic visit.[52]

Tanaka's diplomatic gamble with China was made possible by the strategic space afforded internationally by a shift in the balance of the US–Soviet–China triangle. On the one hand was the thaw in US–Soviet relations. The core of this US–Soviet detente was the effort by Washington and Moscow to control the nuclear arms race through the Strategic Arms Limitation Talks (SALT) that began in 1969. The US and the Soviet Union hoped that detente would reduce the risk of nuclear war as well as ease rises in the cost of military spending for both. On the other hand was Nixon's desire to, as he had written in his *Foreign Affairs* article of 1967, end China's 'angry isolation' and 'pull China back into the family of nations'.[53] Nixon viewed repairing US relations with China as essential to global stability given the rising nuclear threat from Beijing and the domestic political chaos in China unleashed by the Cultural Revolution, and as a means to balance US relations with the Soviet Union: 'as I pursue my talks with Soviets, I too might want to keep an anchor to windward with respect to China. In ten years, when China has made significant nuclear progress, we will have no choice.'[54] The sharpening of tensions between China and the Soviet Union towards the end of the 1960s was a strong incentive for China to improve relations with the US. These had led to military clashes on the Sino-Soviet border in 1969 and were such that Mao Zedong feared that the Soviet Union was even considering a nuclear first strike against China.[55]

The difficulties of equidistance

Against this background, Japan would have preferred to have ridden in the United States' slipstream, keeping equal distance between China and the Soviet Union and thus allowing Tokyo to improve relations with both.[56] But this was easier in theory than in practice. China also saw normalisation with Japan as a tool to isolate the Soviet Union at a time when Beijing–Moscow relations were in a deep ideological and geopolitical chill. Warming Sino-Japanese political ties, meanwhile, created strategic alarm in Moscow. This alarm rose further when Japan and China agreed a Treaty of Peace and Friendship, which came into force in 1978 and included the anti-Soviet 'anti-hegemony clause' that the Chinese had requested and the US had encouraged Japan to accept despite Japanese reluctance to do so.[57] From Moscow's point of view, this treaty presented an unappealing alliance of Chinese scale with Japanese tech-nology and wealth. Beijing, meanwhile, sought during the 1970s to obstruct Japan–Soviet economic cooperation and advances in Japan's territorial dispute with the Soviet Union over the Northern Territories/Southern Kuril Islands.[58] This was particularly the case in the immediate period after the confirmation of the anti-Soviet Deng Xiaoping's paramount power over the Chinese Communist Party (CCP) and the state at the Third Plenum of the CCP's 11th Central Committee at the end of 1978.[59] US foreign policy towards China during the administration of president Jimmy Carter in 1977–81, which was animated by its antagonism towards the Soviet Union and overlapped with the Soviet invasion of Afghanistan in 1979, ended detente and further undermined Tokyo's hopes for equidistance.[60] Japan was not powerful enough and too reliant on its alliance with the US to hold its own against this external geopolitical turbulence.

Chinese domestic political instability at the tail end of the Cultural Revolution in the run-up to and immediate aftermath of Mao's death in 1976 also limited the immediate economic gains to Japan from normalisation. These had to wait until Deng's consolidation of power and his active solicitation of foreign capital for China's economy through his 'Open Door' reforms. Following the signing of the Sino-Japanese Treaty of Peace and Friendship in 1978 and with the additional tailwind of the normalisation of Sino-US relations in 1979, Japan became an active financial contributor to modernising

China's economic base, with Tokyo hoping that a stronger Chinese economy would both contribute to Chinese political stability and yield commercial opportunities for Japanese business.

The Sino-Japanese golden age

From 1979, when prime minister Ohira Masayoshi announced during a visit to Beijing that Japan would give financial assistance to China, until the end of the aid programme in 2008, Japan gave ¥3 trillion (US$30 billion) of assistance in the form of low-interest loans, grants and technical cooperation.[61] With Japanese official development assistance (ODA) providing 40% of the funds for electrification of China's railways and 11% of the funds for additional electric power-generation capacity, Japan played the leading external role in modernising China's economy in this period, also viewing Chinese economic health as vital for regional security.[62] Japan's financial largesse also laid the foundations for the Chinese economic boom that lasted from the late 1990s until the global financial crash of 2008, a bittersweet irony for Japan given China's subsequent transformation into its greatest security threat.

Indeed, prior to the 1989 Beijing Tiananmen Square massacre, the 1980s had been a golden age for Sino-Japanese relations as economic links between the two countries deepened. But Japan was unable to achieve similar balance in its relations with the US and the Soviet Union. During the latter part of the 1980s there was an improvement in relations on all three sides of the US–China–Soviet geopolitical triangle, the first such since the formation of the PRC in 1949. This owed much to the flexibility of the 'new thinking' foreign policy initiated by Soviet leader Mikhail Gorbachev, who took power in 1985.[63] Thus Soviet relations with the US and China improved, and Gorbachev even visited Beijing in 1989, the first visit by a Soviet leader in 20 years.

Japan's relations with the US, already strained by economic

tensions, were aggravated further by the revelations in 1987 of Japanese violations of the rules of the Coordinating Committee for Multilateral Export Controls (COCOM), which was set up in 1949 to prevent the flow of military or dual-use technology to communist countries.[64] Japan's relations with the Soviet Union, meanwhile, were affected by Japanese concerns about Moscow's evolving Asia strategy. This was suggested in a major foreign-policy speech Gorbachev made in Vladivostok in 1986 in which, inter alia, he announced extensive measures to improve relations with China, berated Japan (along with South Korea) for its role in the US-led 'militarized triangle' and for 'circumvent[ing]' 'the peaceful provisions of [its] Constitution', and emphasised the Soviet Union's position as 'an Asian and Pacific country'.[65] But Tokyo was most irked by the lack of any reference to the Northern Territories/ Southern Kurils dispute in the speech, and Gorbachev's desire to deal with Japan 'free from the problems of the past', which in Japan's view meant absent the territorial dispute.[66] He also proposed a conference for Asia along the lines of the European Helsinki Process, which had led to the 1975 Helsinki Final Act.[67] Japan was opposed to the latter, which had been a high point of detente in Europe and had done much to defuse tensions between East and West Europe in the 1970s. This was largely because doing so might entail Japan having to accept international borders as they were, thus forcing Tokyo to give up its Northern Territories/Southern Kurils claim. The change of prime minister in Tokyo in late 1987 from Nakasone to Takeshita Noboru, whose main focus was on domestic politics, acted as a further brake on Japan–Soviet relations. Rather than exploiting the new Soviet diplomatic openness, Takeshita's government preferred to focus on the territorial dispute.[68]

Abe's Russia policy: failure and prescience

Tokyo's attempt to triangulate its relationship with China and Russia in order to boost Japanese security was evident more recently during prime minister Abe's second term. Abe pursued a two-pronged policy towards Beijing and Moscow to try and prevent Sino-Russian strategic alignment. Towards the former, while recognising the economic necessity for Japan to have close relations with China, he understood that successfully navigating relations with China also required dealing with it from a position of reinvigorated national strength.[69] This need to strengthen Japanese power informed his internal balancing to strengthen Japan's relative economic and military positions, which included his 'Abenomics' economic programme, his defence reforms, and his external balancing through, for example, deploying Japan's geo-economic power. One leading example of the latter came in the form of his administration's support for the survival of the Trans-Pacific Partnership (TPP) mega trade bloc after the United States' withdrawal from it in 2017. Thanks in large part to Japanese persistence, the TPP was reborn as the Comprehensive and Progressive Agreement for Trans-Pacific Partnership (CPTPP) in 2018. The CPTPP has since become an important tool for geo-economic rule-making in the region.

Towards Moscow, meanwhile, in his second term Abe showed considerable forbearance at a time of rising geopolitical tensions between Russia and the US and Europe. Making progress on the territorial dispute with Russia over the Habomai Islands, and three other islands, Shikotan, Kunashiri and Etorofu – that is, the Northern Territories/Southern Kurils – was one policy priority for Abe. Abe *père*, Abe Shintaro, had played a key role as foreign minister in prime minister Nakasone's attempt to resolve the territorial dispute as part of what Nakasone viewed as settling the remaining legacy issues from the Second World War.[70] Abe *fils* also saw the restoration to Japanese sovereignty as part of Japan's full emergence from the constraints of the post-Second World War settlement – in his memoirs, for example, published posthumously, he groups the issue in a chapter concerned with resolution of post-war foreign-policy legacy issues.[71]

To this end, in 2018 he moderated Japan's position on the dispute, proposing to Russia negotiations based on a return to the Joint Declaration by the Union of Soviet Socialist Republics and Japan of 1956. The Declaration had ended the state of war between Japan and the Soviet Union and agreed that the latter would transfer to Japan two of the four disputed territories, the Habomai Islands and Shikotan, after the signing of a bilateral peace treaty.[72] Bilateral positions on the issue, however, hardened with the 1960 revision to the US–Japan security treaty, with, for example, the Soviet Union demanding the withdrawal of foreign military forces from Japan as a precondition for proceeding with the terms of the Declaration.[73] Under Abe's new plan, Japan would contribute along with Russia, meanwhile, to 'joint economic activities' on the two other (and largest) of the disputed territories, Etorofu and Kunashiri.[74] Japan's full support for US-led punitive sanctions against Russia have, however, in effect frozen Japan–Russia relations, Japan's continued energy project in Sakhalin notwithstanding. Moreover, Japan has since reverted to the description of the islands as the 'inherent territory of Japan' (*Nihon koyū no ryōdo*), a stronger formulation that had not been used officially since 2011.[75]

While Abe's pro-Russia policy failed, his understanding that closer relations between China and Russia constitute a danger to Japan was prescient.[76] Sino-Russian strategic cooperation was evident before 2022 – the two countries' joint naval patrol around three of Japan's main islands, Honshu, Shikoku and Kyushu, in 2021 was once such example.[77] Sino-Russian strategic alignment has intensified since 2022, with further joint patrols, both by sea and by air. Russian warships have also been reported off the coast of Taiwan.[78] Although these bilateral patrols are not integrated, they are designed to send a strong political message to Japan, its ally the US and its partners. The 'Defense of Japan 2024' white paper from Japan's Ministry of Defense notes this cooperation as a 'demonstration of force against Japan' and describes it as of 'grave concern from the perspective of the national security of Japan'.[79]

Complementing this have been the deepening trade links between Russia and China as a result of the US-led coalition's efforts to escalate sanctions against Russia since its invasion of Ukraine. These sanctions have forced Russia's economy, which even before 2022 was the largest economy to have been sanctioned in peacetime, to reorient towards China since 2022.[80] Even in the event of a sustainable cessation of hostilities between Russia and Ukraine, rising economic-security concerns in the EU and a successful weaning of EU energy supply off Russian hydrocarbons suggest that this market is lost to Russia on a permanent basis. Russia's broader strategic switch to China thus now looks like a structural rather than a temporary phenomenon. This, coupled with Russia's tightening security links with North Korea, which is also China's only treaty ally, means that Japan faces an arc of threat stretching from its northern to its southern flanks. Small wonder then that Japan's 2022 National Security Strategy highlights the 'historical changes in power balances and intensifying geopolitical competitions' in its very first paragraph.[81]

CHAPTER TWO

Building Japanese deterrence and response capabilities – defence and diplomacy

Intentions are profoundly important in a strategic context where countries can only be protected against the malign intentions of others by the functioning of a deterrence system anchored on the threat of retaliation.[1]

Colin S. Gray, *The Geopolitics of Super Power*, 1988

Change is coming that hasn't happened in 100 years. And we're driving this change together.[2]

**Chinese President Xi Jinping to Russian President Vladimir Putin
in 2023 at the end of Xi's visit to Moscow**

Changing defence assumptions

The deterioration in Japan's external environment since 2010 has wrought two major interrelated changes on its assumptions about the military pillar of its grand strategy. The first relates to the purpose of the United States–Japan security alliance, the cornerstone of Japanese security. During the Cold War, the alliance was designed primarily to support US military efforts in the event of a broad regional conflict. This was most likely as part of a conflict with the Soviet Union, but also of actual and potential conflicts elsewhere in the region.[3] In the 1990s, after the end of the Cold War and with initial hopes that Russia might become a benign international actor, the alliance switched its strategic focus to the United States' defence of South Korea. The evolving threat from the early 1990s on the Korean Peninsula associated with North Korea's nuclear-weapons programme made this switch necessary, and forced operational changes to the alliance.

In 1992–94, during the first North Korean nuclear crisis, Pyongyang announced its intention to leave the Nuclear Non-Proliferation Treaty (NPT), which mandates non-nuclear-weapons state signatories not to manufacture nuclear weapons. In the lead-up to this crisis, North Korea refused access to its suspect nuclear-waste site to inspectors from the International Atomic Energy Agency. In 1994, the US even considered military action against Pyongyang to stop its nuclear programme.[4] The North Korean threat spurred a revision in 1997 of the Guidelines for Japan–US Defense Cooperation, which provide the operational framework for the US–Japan security alliance. The 1997 revision was the first such since the guidelines were issued in 1978, and, notably, the new parameters expanded the focus of the alliance from the defence of Japan in the original version to 'areas surrounding Japan', reflecting the need to take account of the North Korean threat.[5]

In recent years, however, the strategic focus of the alliance has grown to include the defence of Taiwan against a potential Chinese attack. As noted in the Introduction, China's increasingly belligerent rhetoric and actions regarding its intentions towards the island, and Beijing's sustained investment in expanding its force-projection capabilities, have necessitated this change in focus. As a result, in the words of Japanese defence-affairs scholar Michishita Narushige, 'the US–Japan alliance is now committed to the defence of South Korea and Taiwan simultaneously'.[6] It is against this background that the historic programme of defence reforms announced in the end-2022 National Security Strategy (NSS), which include the pledge to increase the defence budget from around 1% of GDP to 2% by fiscal year 2027–28, should be seen.

The second change to Japan's assumptions about its grand strategy relates to the increasing likelihood that Japan itself may be attacked. For Japan this is an important strategic and even emotional shift, signalling the end of what Japanese defence scholar and military historian Chijiwa Yasuaki describes as one of the distinctive features (*Nihonteki kannen*) of Japan's post-war understanding of the bilateral alliance, that is, Japanese 'unilateral pacifism' (*ikkoku heiwashugi*), or the notion that Japan can stand aside from conflicts.[7] During the Cold War, the principal security threat to Japan came from the Soviet Union. In this period, China was too weak to constitute a direct security threat to Japan. During the golden period of Sino-Japanese ties in the 1980s, China also even flirted with the notion of bilateral security cooperation with Japan.[8] The nature of the Soviet threat to Japan did not, however, lead to a switch in public opinion in favour of a dramatic change in Japan's own defence policies. This suggested confidence in the ability of the security alliance with the US to protect Japan and a view that any attack on Japan would come as part of a broader conflict rather than be directed specifically at Japan.[9]

North Korea's advancing weapons programme and test firing of missiles in Japan's direction have sharpened Japanese fears of a direct attack. Some of Pyongyang's test launches have even overflown Japan, as happened in 2017 and 2022.[10] Japanese concerns have been amplified by heightened China–Taiwan tensions and the impact of this on maritime stability near Japan. As part of its response to the visit to Taiwan in 2022 by then-speaker of the US House of Representatives Nancy Pelosi (see Introduction), China fired without warning five ballistic missiles into the waters of Japan's exclusive economic zone (EEZ) not far from Taiwan, albeit an EEZ that China disputes.[11] This was also the first time that a Chinese missile had landed in Japan's EEZ and a potent reminder of the vulnerability of Japanese territory should there be a Chinese attack on Taiwan. Small wonder, then, that Tokyo has fears of Japanese territory sustaining collateral damage should there be a war between

China and Taiwan, or even of an attempt to neutralise Japanese assets in this strategically important area. The building of bomb shelters on Japanese territory closest to Taiwan and the plans for evacuation of civilians in such a scenario – a live issue that is now frequently reported in the mainstream Japanese media – are reflections of this.[12]

Japan's strategic shift to the Southwest Islands

It is difficult to overemphasise Taiwan's strategic importance to the US–Japan alliance and to Japan itself, or Japan's potential role in helping to defend Taiwan against Chinese attack. As *The Economist* noted in 2021 in an article on Taiwan-related tensions and their impact on Japan's southwestern region, no country 'except perhaps Taiwan itself, has as much influence as Japan over how it will unfold – nor as much to lose if it goes badly'.[13] As set out in the Introduction, Japan would be one of the major geopolitical losers were China successful in absorbing Taiwan by force.

Viewed in this light, the priority given to the defence of Japan's southwestern region in the end-2022 NSS documents makes strategic sense. This area constitutes a good half of the northern portion of the first island chain of the East China Sea and, as such, is highly likely to be involved in the event of a full-scale Chinese attack on Taiwan. This could either be by accident given the region's geographical proximity to Taiwan, or by design. The region would be a key part of any Chinese anti-access/area-denial (A2/AD) strategy to prevent the US from coming to Taiwan's aid and thus a strategic target for China. In this scenario, Japan is likely to come under pressure from the US to deploy its SSK diesel-electric attack submarines at the choke points of the region to prevent Chinese forces from breaking out into the Pacific to challenge US forces in the area.[14] With this threat in mind, in 2018 the Japan Self-Defense Forces (SDF) created an Amphibious Rapid Deployment Brigade, Japan's first such since the end of the Second World War, as a 'Japanese marine corps'.[15] Tokyo has also been building up assets to deny adversaries entry into Japan's maritime territory, including destroyers, submarines and patrol aircraft.[16]

As part of Japan's strategic geographical refocus, the SDF is already moving military resources southwards from the northernmost main island of Hokkaido, where they had been concentrated since the Cold War to counter the then-Soviet threat (see Map 7).[17] This redeployment is also part of what the Defense Buildup Program notes as the deepening of 'joint flexible deterrent options' alongside the US. Even before 2022, however, Japan had been building out its defence capabilities in the southwestern region. In 2013, for example, there were SDF facilities at 39 locations on the Nansei Islands; by 2023, this had risen to 57 locations.[18]

The strategic task for Japan is, however, immense, reflecting both the vastness of the region and its proximity to Taiwan. Ishigaki Island, for example, lies nearly 2,000 kilometres from Tokyo and just over 400 km from Okinawa's capital, Naha, but only 170 km from the disputed Senkaku/Diaoyu Islands and just under 300 km from Taiwan.[19] The whole region, which stretches from the southern tip of the southernmost main island of Kyushu to the vicinity of Taiwan, is as long as Japan's main island of Honshu, adding to concerns about Japan's ability to supply the region smoothly in the event of a conflict.[20]

As part of the reinforcement of the southwestern region and strengthening of Japan's deterrence capabilities, the end-2022 NSS included some eye-catching proposals. One was the intro-duction of counterstrike capabilities for Japan, a development made necessary by the expanding missile gap in the region between China and North Korea on the one hand, and Japan and the US on the other. An assessment by the US Department

Map 7: **Selected changes to Japan's force posture in Kyushu and the southwestern region since 2016**

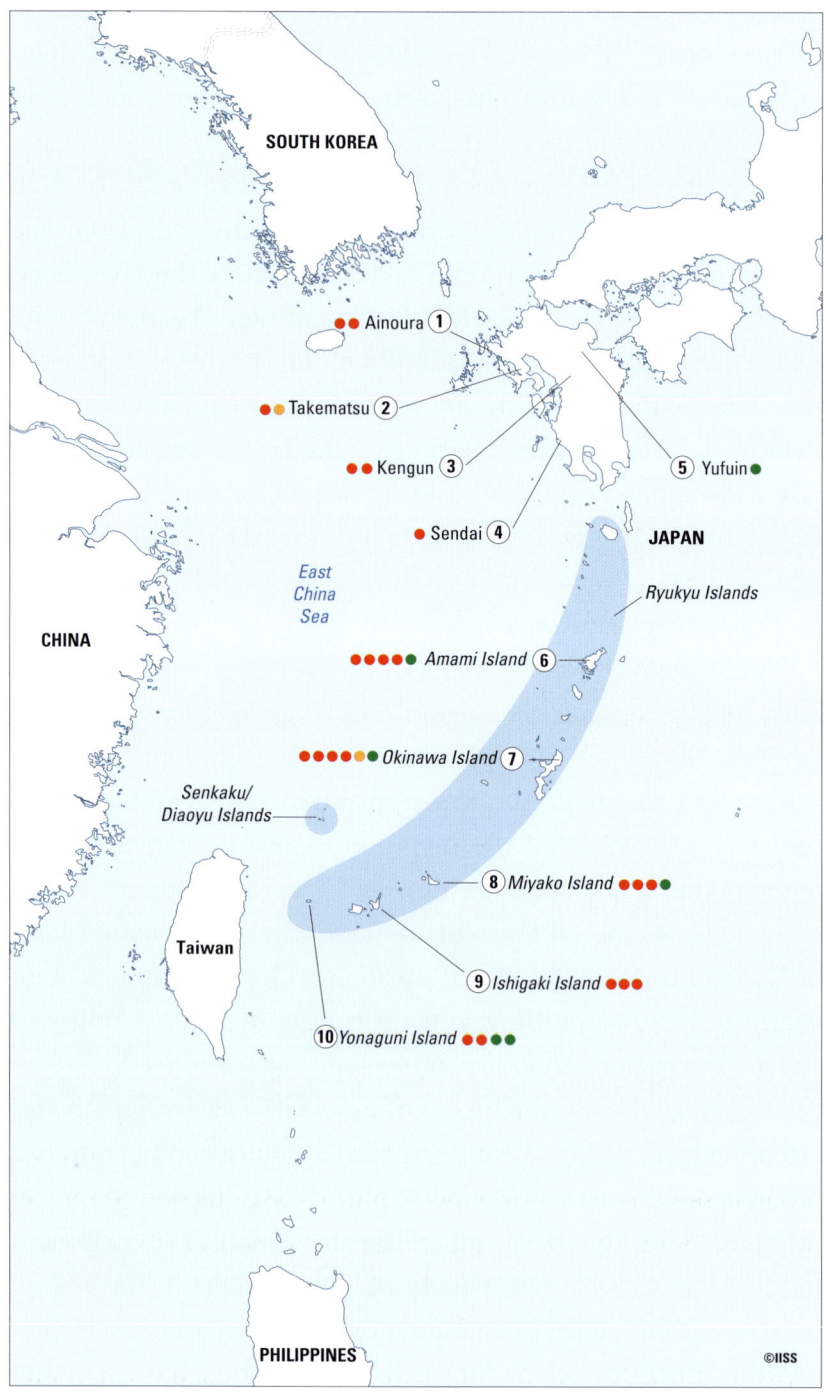

Location	Established between 2016 and April 2023	Established April 2023–April 2024	Planned
(1) Ainoura	● 2018 JGSDF Amphibious Rapid Deployment Brigade		
	● 2022 JGSDF EW unit		
(2) Takematsu	● 2022 JGSDF SAM unit	● 2024 JGSDF 3rd Amphibious Rapid Deployment Regiment	
(3) Kengun	● 2021 JGSDF EW unit		
	● 2022 JGSDF AShM unit		
(4) Sendai	● 2023 JGSDF EW unit		
(5) Yufuin			● JGSDF AShM unit
(6) *Amami Island*	● 2019 JGSDF Amami area security unit		● Ammunition-storage facility
	● 2019 JGSDF SAM unit		
	● 2019 JGSDF AShM unit		
	● 2022 JGSDF EW unit		
(7) *Okinawa Island*	● 2016 JASDF Air Wing	● 2024 JGSDF AShM unit	● Reorganisation of JGSDF 15th Brigade into division-sized unit
	● 2017 JASDF Southwestern Air Defense Force		
	● 2017 Southwestern Aircraft Control and Warning Wing		
	● 2022 JGSDF EW unit		
(8) *Miyako Island*	● 2019 JGSDF Miyako area security unit		● JGSDF EW unit
	● 2020 JGSDF AShM unit		
	● 2020 JGSDF SAM unit (redeployed)		
(9) *Ishigaki Island*	● 2023 JGSDF Yaeyama area security unit		
	● 2023 JGSDF AShM unit		
	● 2023 JGSDF SAM unit		
(10) *Yonaguni Island*	● 2016 JGSDF Yonaguni Coast Observation unit		● JGSDF EW unit
	● 2022 JASDF Warning Squadron (part deployed)		● JGSDF SAM unit

AShM: anti-ship missile; **EW**: electronic warfare; **SAM**: surface-to-air missile; **JGSDF**: Japan Ground Self-Defense Force; **JASDF**: Japan Air Self-Defense Force
Note: Precise unit sizes are unclear.
Sources: Defense of Japan 2023 (Annual White Paper); Japan Ministry of Defense

of Defense reckons that China has some 2,000 ballistic and cruise missiles capable of reaching Japanese territory, while Japan is seeking to acquire more than 1,500 of its own stand-off missiles, both US *Tomahawk* cruise missiles and domestically developed missiles.[21]

The debate over Japanese counterstrike capability is not new – prime minister Hatoyama Ichiro considered the capability to fall within the parameters of Japan's constitutional constraints as far back as 1956.[22] The 2018 National Defense Program Guidelines also argued the case for 'stand-off defense capability'.[23] But the 2022 commitment to 'enable Japan to mount effective counterstrikes against the opponent to prevent further attacks' and to disrupt aggressor activity earlier and further from Japan is a significant doctrinal departure for Japan.[24] The Japanese government is at pains to emphasise that this and other reforms sit within existing constitutional constraints – stating, for example, that 'counterstrike capabilities fall within the purview of Japan's Constitution and international law; they do not change Japan's exclusively defense-oriented policy'.[25] That the government is able to do so also reflects the increasingly blurred distinction between defence and offence, given the impact of advanced technology on modern warfare.

But here, too, the headwinds are significant. For one thing, building counterstrike capabilities will consume considerable resources from an already strained Japanese budget – some ¥5 trillion (US$34 billion) in the years to 2027.[26] With this shift Japan is also committing itself to a 'forward-leaning denial strategy' that constitutes a considerable challenge for Japan in terms of both logistics and capabilities.[27] It is also a major shift from Japan's existing missile-defence architecture, which has relied on intercepting missiles through ballistic-missile defence systems.[28] Map 8 gives an overview of selected Japanese missile programmes.

Japan's counterstrike capability also requires closer cooperation and integration between Japan and the US to coordinate deployment, for example in space from the point of view of information-gathering, communications and positioning in support of Japan being able to deploy this capability.[29] The United States' plan, announced in July 2024, to upgrade its military command in Japan to a joint-force

Map 8: **Selected Japanese missile programmes**

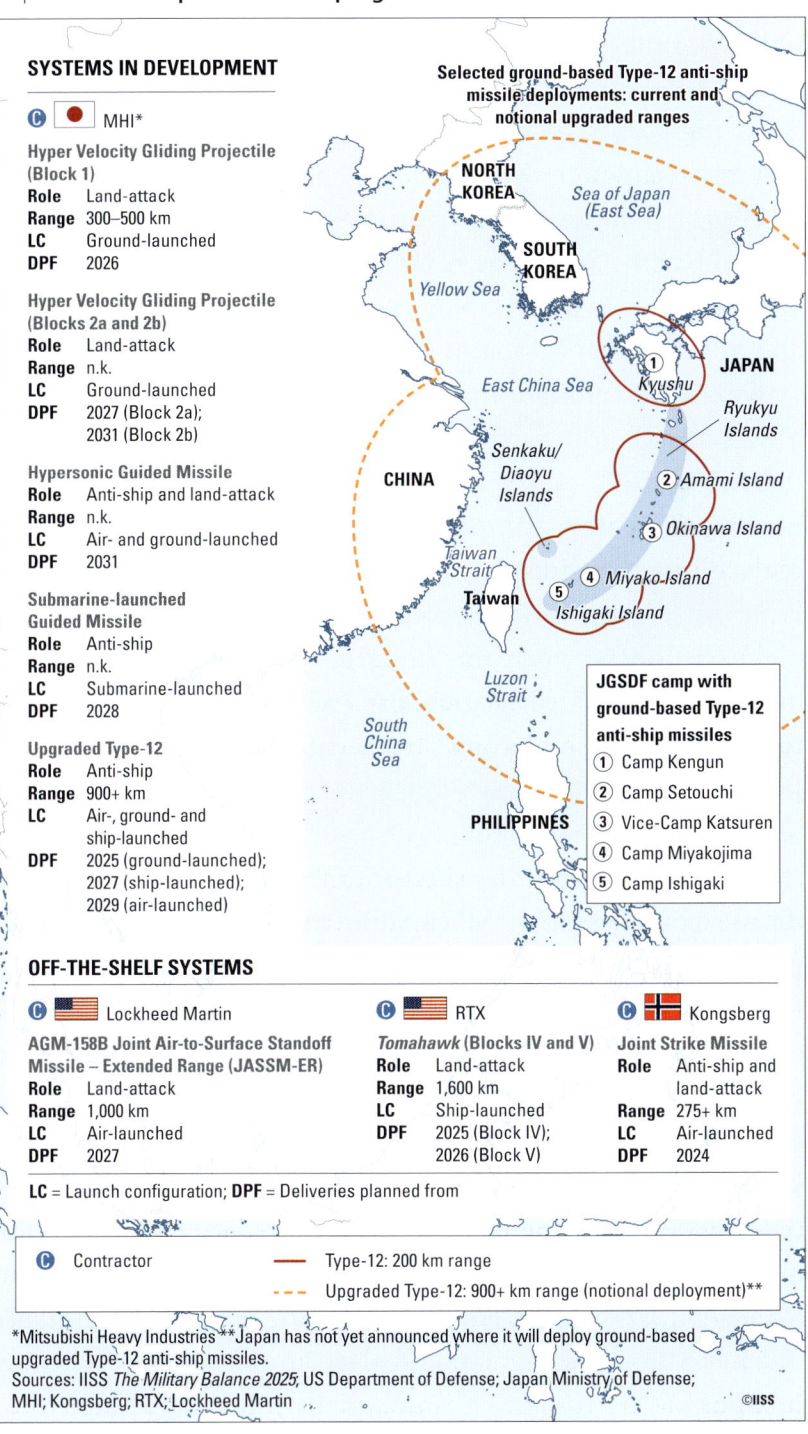

SYSTEMS IN DEVELOPMENT

Ⓒ 🔴 MHI*

Hyper Velocity Gliding Projectile (Block 1)
Role	Land-attack
Range	300–500 km
LC	Ground-launched
DPF	2026

Hyper Velocity Gliding Projectile (Blocks 2a and 2b)
Role	Land-attack
Range	n.k.
LC	Ground-launched
DPF	2027 (Block 2a); 2031 (Block 2b)

Hypersonic Guided Missile
Role	Anti-ship and land-attack
Range	n.k.
LC	Air- and ground-launched
DPF	2031

Submarine-launched Guided Missile
Role	Anti-ship
Range	n.k.
LC	Submarine-launched
DPF	2028

Upgraded Type-12
Role	Anti-ship
Range	900+ km
LC	Air-, ground- and ship-launched
DPF	2025 (ground-launched); 2027 (ship-launched); 2029 (air-launched)

Selected ground-based Type-12 anti-ship missile deployments: current and notional upgraded ranges

NORTH KOREA
Sea of Japan (East Sea)
SOUTH KOREA
Yellow Sea
East China Sea
JAPAN
① Kyushu
Ryukyu Islands
Senkaku/ Diaoyu Islands
CHINA
② Amami Island
③ Okinawa Island
Taiwan Strait
④ Miyako Island
⑤ Ishigaki Island
Taiwan
Luzon Strait
South China Sea
PHILIPPINES

JGSDF camp with ground-based Type-12 anti-ship missiles
① Camp Kengun
② Camp Setouchi
③ Vice-Camp Katsuren
④ Camp Miyakojima
⑤ Camp Ishigaki

OFF-THE-SHELF SYSTEMS

Ⓒ 🇺🇸 Lockheed Martin

AGM-158B Joint Air-to-Surface Standoff Missile – Extended Range (JASSM-ER)
Role	Land-attack
Range	1,000 km
LC	Air-launched
DPF	2027

Ⓒ 🇺🇸 RTX

***Tomahawk* (Blocks IV and V)**
Role	Land-attack
Range	1,600 km
LC	Ship-launched
DPF	2025 (Block IV); 2026 (Block V)

Ⓒ 🇳🇴 Kongsberg

Joint Strike Missile
Role	Anti-ship and land-attack
Range	275+ km
LC	Air-launched
DPF	2024

LC = Launch configuration; **DPF** = Deliveries planned from

Ⓒ Contractor

—— Type-12: 200 km range

- - - Upgraded Type-12: 900+ km range (notional deployment)**

*Mitsubishi Heavy Industries **Japan has not yet announced where it will deploy ground-based upgraded Type-12 anti-ship missiles.
Sources: IISS *The Military Balance 2025*; US Department of Defense; Japan Ministry of Defense; MHI; Kongsberg; RTX; Lockheed Martin

©IISS

headquarters headed by a three-star general and reporting to the commander of Indo-Pacific Command was a reflection of the need for closer integration between the two allies. In 2024, then US secretary of defense Lloyd Austin described this move as 'the most significant change to US Forces Japan since its creation'.[30] The United States' reorganisation will dovetail with Japan's own plan to set up a Permanent Joint Headquarters to unify Japan's Air, Ground and Maritime SDF and to be headed by a joint-service commander.

Increasing cross-domain operations have made having a structured approach to inter-service cooperation essential for the SDF. Hitherto, cooperation has been on an ad hoc basis, creating complexity in chains of command. Inter-service mistrust in the Imperial Japanese armed forces crippled strategy in the Second World War. Witness the strategic friction between the Imperial Japanese Navy's desire to advance southwards into the Pacific and Southeast Asia to use its amphibious and blue-water capabilities, and the Imperial Japanese Army's push for a northern advance into Siberia and northern China.[31] Or the concealing by the former from the latter of its aircraft-carrier losses after the Japanese defeat at the Battle of Midway in 1942.[32] Clearly, much has changed since then, but closer inter-service cooperation within the SDF will still require a change of mindset, which may take time.[33] These efforts to upgrade the two countries' command-and-control functions also underscore how far expectations of Japan's contribution to the security relationship with the US have changed from Japan taking a purely defensive role in any contingency. That said, the creation of a joint US–Japanese command along the lines of the South Korea–US Combined Forces Command still looks unlikely given the lingering legal, political and public-opinion barriers in Japan.

Building defence and defence-industrial resilience

Another important aspect of the 2022 NSS was the focus on building Japanese defence resilience. Again, this is sound strategy given the likelihood that a conflict with China over Taiwan would be protracted. The full-scale war between Russia and Ukraine that started in 2022 has been catastrophic for both countries in terms of blood spilled and treasure lost. But it has provided insights into how inter-state warfare has evolved in a world in which emerging technologies such as artificial intelligence (AI), cyber and space technology have also been weaponised.

Despite the topographical differences between Ukraine and Taiwan, Chinese President Xi Jinping will surely have drawn two lessons for China from Russia's experience in the war: firstly, that China would hope to win any full-scale war with Taiwan at speed, that is, before the US or Japan could mobilise a response; and secondly, that China would also need to prepare for an extended conflict, as has become the case with Russia's war on Ukraine. The latter may be more likely, as one observer notes: 'exhaustion of morale and matériel rather than finality through battle marks the endgame of many wars. Even of most wars.'[34]

Indeed, China's geographical proximity to Taiwan may well give China an advantage in such a conflict in terms of speed, particularly if the US was reluctant to attack China itself. Relatedly, added to the strategic complexity of dealing with a Taiwan contingency for Japan and the US is the time it would take the US to move its military assets fully into the region. The question of how long Japan would be able to hold out until the US arrived in force thus looms large. Estimates vary as to how long it would need to hold out, depending on the scale of the United States' military response, from a matter of days to several weeks.[35]

For Japanese defence resilience, this creates multiple challenges. One is logistical. As already outlined, Japan's geography is elongated, meaning that distances are long. Moreover, some 60% of Japan's land is covered by mountains. This topography would complicate the moving of supplies during a conflict, especially if Japanese territory also came under attack. Given the deepening strategic cooperation between China, Russia and North Korea, Japanese territory might also be threatened along its full length, should Pyongyang and Moscow launch supporting operations on the Korean Peninsula and on Japan's northern flank. The Japanese government is therefore seeking as a matter of urgency to harden its airports and seaports 'with a view to responding to contingencies'.[36] Given the importance of the Southwestern Islands, the government has a strategic focus on infrastructure located on Japan's southern flank, on the main islands of Kyushu and Shikoku.[37]

Another challenge is the stockpiling of ammunition. Japan's stocks of ammunition have run low over the years, compromising its 'fighting ability' (keisen nōryoku). An article in Japan's leading financial daily newspaper, Nihon Keizai Shimbun, in 2022 indicated that the government reckoned that Japan has only 60% of the ammunition that it would need for a three-month-long defence of the southwestern region and that the government plans to establish production facilities to fill the gap.[38] Japan's geography means that it lacks strategic depth. This means in turn that it also needs to both increase and disperse the number of ammunition-storage facilities, again with a focus on ensuring the supply to the southwestern region.[39]

This shines a glaring light on the broader weakness in Japan's defence-industrial base. Reflecting the legacy of the Yoshida Doctrine and the lack of a diversified clientele, defence has long been the 'Cinderella sector' of Japanese industry.

As a result, unlike its counterparts in, say, the US, the United Kingdom and the European Union, Japan's defence sector lacks scale and is fragmented. The problems in the sector are evident in its shrinkage in recent years – in the first two decades or so of this century, some 100 companies have left the sector.[40] Between 2014 and 2023, domestic procurement fell as a share of Japan's defence budget from 89.3% to 76.5%.[41]

The government hopes that the progressive loosening of the politically imposed constraints on exports of defence equipment, and collaborative projects such as the UK–Italy–Japan Global Combat Aircraft Programme (GCAP – announced in December 2022 and with the new aircraft scheduled to come into service by 2035), will help to raise the sector's competitiveness.[42] Japan has also been pursuing greater defence-industrial cooperation with the US. In 2024, the two countries launched the Defense Industrial Cooperation, Acquisition, and Sustainment (DICAS) meeting. The DICAS forum is intended to identify areas for closer defence-equipment policy collaboration against the background of the easing of Japanese defence-export constraints, and is an important extension to existing US–Japan dialogue in areas such as technology.[43] Closer US–Japan defence-industrial links, meanwhile, are also designed to buttress US strategic capacity against a background of multiplying global calls on US military resources.[44]

Cyber, intelligence and space

Japan's ability to contribute to the security of Taiwan will also hinge on its intelligence, surveillance and reconnaissance (ISR) abilities, particularly given its stated desire to disrupt potential enemies 'at further distance' than hitherto. Japan's first NSS, in 2013, recognised the strategic importance of space and cyberspace as critical areas of national security for Japan, as well as the need for Japan to cooperate with the US in these areas.[45]

Of the two areas, Japan's space programme is the most evolved, reflecting the spur to development from two strategic shocks to Tokyo: the '*Taepodong* shock' of 1998, when a North Korean ballistic missile overflew Japan's largest island of Honshu; and China's successful anti-satellite (ASAT) missile test in 2007, in which it successfully shot down one of its own weather satellites, creating substantial in-orbit debris and threatening Japan's own satellites.[46]

Considerable legal and institutional changes in recent years have supported the expansion of Japanese space capabilities. Japan's Basic Space Law of 2008 allowed for the use of space for 'defensive' purposes, upending the norms of the Peaceful Purposes Resolution of 1969, which stipulated that Japan's space activities be 'limited to peaceful purposes' and be 'non-aggressive' and 'non-military'.[47] A number of developments since then have reinforced the strategic position of space capabilities within Japan's national-security framework. These include the creation of the National Security Council (NSC) in 2013; the passage of the Protection of Specially Designated Secrets Law in the same year;[48] the passage in 2014 of the Basic Act on Cybersecurity, which enabled the launch in 2015 of the Cyber Security Strategy Headquarters under the cabinet; the intention set out in the 2018 National Defense Program Guidelines to 'build a structure to conduct persistent ground- and space-based situation monitoring' and to create a Space Domain Mission Unit; and a number of revisions to Japan's Basic Space Plan, which was first issued in 2009.[49] Japan's strategic focus on space also honours the letter of the 2015 Guidelines for Japan–US Defense Cooperation, which call for bilateral cooperation on space as well as 'seamless' bilateral security and defence cooperation.[50]

Japan's pledge in the 2022 NSS to introduce 'active cyber defence for eliminating in advance the possibility of serious cyberattacks' on Japan's critical infrastructure and networks is another radical departure from Japan's post-war constraints on the 'offensive' use of force.[51] Japan has struggled to match its prowess in commercialising certain cutting-edge technologies with formidable cyber security. This is owing in part to the constraint imposed by Article 21 of Japan's constitution, which protects 'the secrecy of any means of communication', inhibiting the government's ability to gather signals intelligence (SIGINT) despite its SIGINT capabilities.[52] A number of high-profile hacking attacks on Japanese companies in recent years have also spotlit the weakness of corporate Japan's cyber defences, with many companies unwilling to meet the costs of building adequate cyber resilience.[53]

The lack of staff with the requisite skills is also an issue for some of Japan's companies, as it is for the government.[54] One example of the latter is the hurdle that the Japanese Ministry of Defense (JMOD) faces in its plan to quadruple the number of staff working on cyber security to 4,000 by fiscal year 2027–28. This is a tall order given that there are only around 100 people being trained at the SDF's System and Signal/Cyber School.[55] In its 2021 study comparing national cyber power, the IISS ranked Japan in the third tier of countries reviewed, reflecting these and other vulnerabilities.[56] The Japanese government is, however, active in international cyber diplomacy, for example with NATO, the EU and in bilateral cyber dialogues, and capacity-building with regional organisations such as the Association of Southeast Asian Nations (ASEAN).

The 2022 NSS also recognises 'intelligence' specifically as a pillar of Japan's 'comprehensive national power'. Japan's intelligence community is, however, 'very small but complicated', and there is no comprehensive foreign-intelligence organisation such as the CIA in the US or SIS in the UK.[57] There are six agencies in total, with the JMOD's Defense Intelligence

Headquarters (DIH) being the largest, but still far smaller than the National Security Agency in the US, to which some compare it.[58] This has much to do with Japan's post-war demilitarisation and associated normative allergy to clandestine intelligence-gathering and covert foreign operations. Espionage had played an important role in Japan's imperial expansion in Asia before and during the Second World War, and information control had been a key tool for political repression by Japan's military-led governments in the period.[59] This in turn has forced Japan to rely on human intelligence (HUMINT) gathering from, for example, Japanese diplomats as well as international partners such as the US.[60] As the IISS's net assessment of cyber capabilities notes, Japan's cyber-intelligence capabilities remain 'embryonic' and reliant on international partners.[61]

The Designated State Secrets Law mentioned above was an important initiative to protect state secrets and to enable the exchange of military intelligence and defence-industrial information with the US and other partners. The setting up of the NSC in 2013 and the National Security Secretariat, the NSC's 'intelligence coordination unit', in 2014 has also contributed to the easing of competition between agencies and ministries and boosted the government's crisis-management ability.[62] Moreover, the National Security Secretariat's focus on the quality of information received and the input of this information into government policy decisions has also fed back into raising the performance of the providing agencies.[63]

One scholar on Japanese intelligence issues, Richard Samuels, has also drawn attention to the 'tantalising possibility' that the International Counter-Terrorism Intelligence Collection Unit (known as the CTU-J) might one day form the nucleus of a comprehensive intelligence agency given its current international focus, and notes that there are advocates for this in government and in the Liberal Democratic Party (LDP).[64]

There are also voices in Tokyo arguing for Japan to join the Five Eyes intelligence-collaboration group that comprises Australia, Canada, New Zealand, the UK and the US.[65] While Japan would bring to the table advanced technology expertise and additional geographical coverage in a geopolitically tense region, the issues outlined above with its cyber-security and broader intelligence community suggest that this remains some way off. Japan is also building cooperative networks separately with Five Eyes countries.

The mooted expansion of Pillar 2 of the AUKUS security partnership between Australia, the UK and the US to include Japan would be one example of this.[66] Pillar 1 focuses on supporting Australia's acquisition of nuclear-powered submarines, so presents political issues for Japan, not least because of opposition in Japan to using nuclear power for military ends. But Pillar 2 focuses on advanced technologies such as AI and quantum, to which Japan could make a strong contribution. In mid-2024, meanwhile, Japan and New Zealand agreed in principle to share intelligence as part of moves towards a broader information-security agreement.[67] Japan also has intelligence-sharing agreements with Australia, India, South Korea, the UK, the US and NATO and is in discussions on the same with Canada.

Defence diplomacy – networking deterrence

Japan also has been seeking to amplify its own deterrence capabilities in the region through active defence diplomacy. This serves two main functions. The first is to hedge against Japan's perennial fears of a decline in US strategic interest in the region. Since the end of the Second World War, Japan, like other allies of the US, has wavered between fears of entrapment in US wars on the one hand and abandonment by Washington on the other. Given the unpredictability and inward drift of US domestic politics, the predominant concern now is abandonment. The second is to create sufficient strategic complexity for China to deter Beijing from a full-scale attack on Taiwan. This is also a recognition of the scale of the security challenge from Beijing in the region. China, for example, treats its desire to absorb Taiwan as a domestic legacy issue arising from the Chinese Civil War, which ended in 1949.[68] Japan, however, has sought to internationalise the island's security, drawing attention to the wider regional and global impact of a Taiwan contingency. Hence, for example, the concern about 'the importance of peace and stability across the Taiwan Strait' noted in the Biden–Suga summit of 2021 (see Introduction, p. 32). This was expanded in the 2023 G7 Hiroshima Leaders' Communiqué to an affirmation of the 'peace and stability across the Taiwan Strait as indispensable to security and prosperity in the international community'.[69]

Tokyo's defence networking has been evident most recently in the tightening defence links between Japan and the Philippines. During a visit to Japan in early 2023, Philippines President Ferdinand Marcos Jr indicated that 'it's very hard to imagine a scenario where the Philippines will not somehow get involved' should there be a conflict over Taiwan.[70] This in effect mirrors Japan's concerns about its southwestern region, unsurprisingly so given that the Philippines and the Nansei Islands sit south and north of Taiwan respectively. Like Japan, the Philippines has an increasingly acrimonious territorial dispute with China, over the Second Thomas Shoal, a low-tide elevation in the Spratly Islands in the South China Sea (see Map 2, p. 9). A tribunal at the Permanent Court of Arbitration in The Hague ruled in 2016 that the Second Thomas Shoal (and Mischief Reef and Reed Bank) lies within the Philippines' EEZ, but China disputes this.[71] The Philippines is not the only country in the region with a maritime territorial dispute with China.

Map 9: **China's territorial claims**

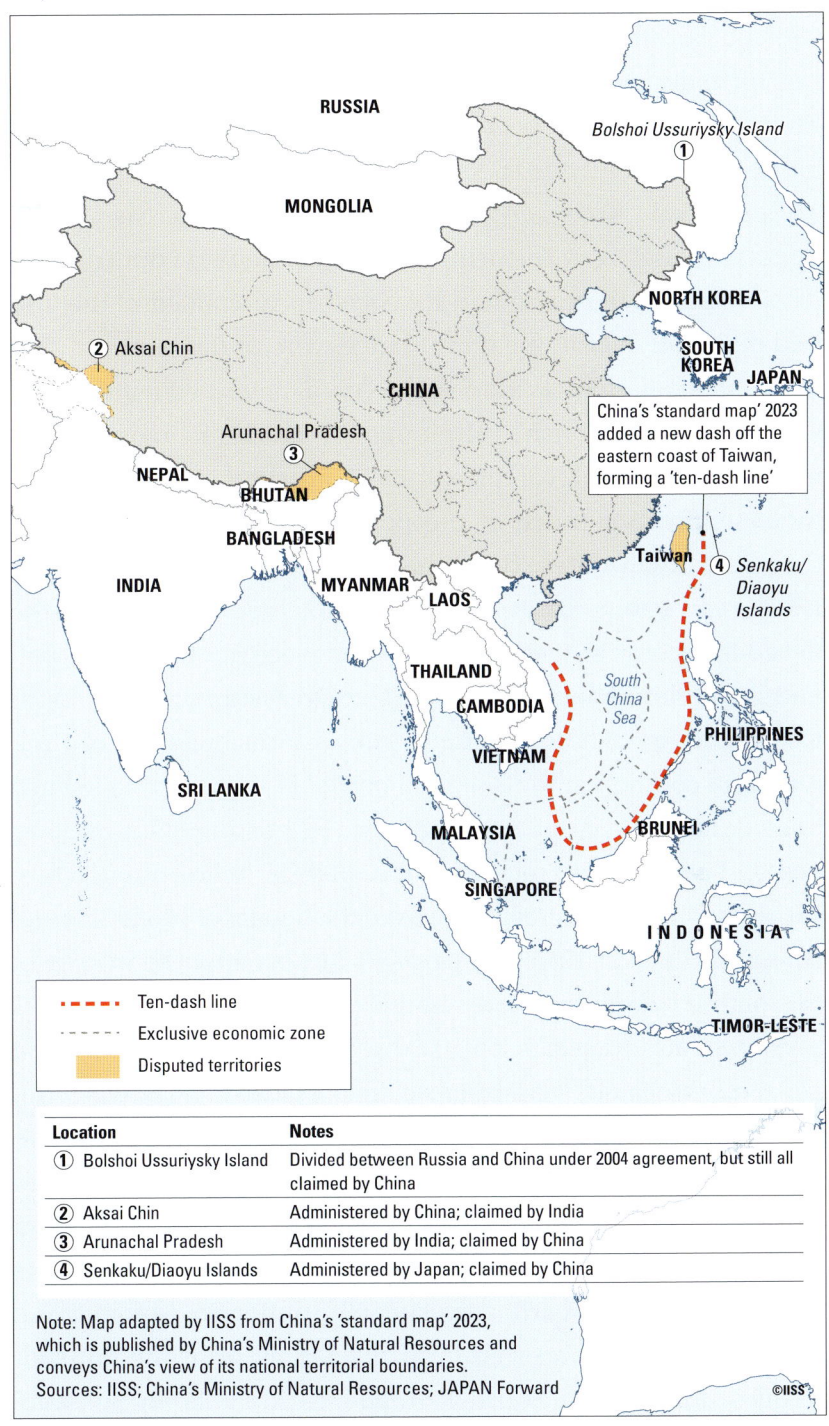

Legend:
- ▬ ▬ ▬ Ten-dash line
- - - - - Exclusive economic zone
- ▨ Disputed territories

China's 'standard map' 2023 added a new dash off the eastern coast of Taiwan, forming a 'ten-dash line'

Location	Notes
① Bolshoi Ussuriysky Island	Divided between Russia and China under 2004 agreement, but still all claimed by China
② Aksai Chin	Administered by China; claimed by India
③ Arunachal Pradesh	Administered by India; claimed by China
④ Senkaku/Diaoyu Islands	Administered by Japan; claimed by China

Note: Map adapted by IISS from China's 'standard map' 2023, which is published by China's Ministry of Natural Resources and conveys China's view of its national territorial boundaries.
Sources: IISS; China's Ministry of Natural Resources; JAPAN Forward

©IISS

Indeed, Beijing claims sovereignty over some 80% of the South China Sea, affecting a number of countries, although it has not formally pressed these claims, and the dispute with the Philippines has so far been the most acrimonious.[72] Against this background, in July 2024, Japan and the Philippines concluded a Reciprocal Access Agreement (RAA) to increase inter-operability between the armed forces of the two countries. As of early 2025, Japan also had RAAs with Australia and the UK, and negotiations for one with France were under way.

Japan's relations with South Korea have been important since the two established diplomatic relations in 1965, reflecting their geographical proximity and overlapping strategic interests. But for much of the period since the emergence of the two Korean states, Tokyo has been able to compartmentalise Korean Peninsula issues. While North Korea has over the decades become a steadily more potent security threat to Japan and the region, Tokyo could take some reassurance from South Korea and its US ally having prime responsibility for dealing with any conflict on the Korean Peninsula. Japan's role in such a scenario would come principally via its hosting of US military bases. Tokyo–Seoul relations, meanwhile, were often whip-sawed by bitter disagreements over the legacy of Japan's brutal colonial rule over Korea in 1910–45, but broadly the impact of this on the balance of power in the region was limited.

However, Russia's full-scale invasion of Ukraine in 2022 transformed the strategic importance of Tokyo–Seoul relations for Japan's grand strategy, contributing to two parallel shifts in the US-led alliance system either side of the Eurasian landmass. One was the accession of Finland and Sweden, both hitherto militarily neutral, to NATO. The former joined in April 2023 and the latter in March 2024. The other was a concerted effort by Japanese prime minister Kishida Fumio and South Korean president Yoon Suk-yeol to repair ties following the chill that had set in from around 2017 as differences over shared history resurfaced. The issue of compensation for the Korean women forced to work in wartime military brothels by the Imperial Japanese Army (the 'comfort women') and for Korean forced labourers were the main causes of the deterioration in bilateral relations.

The rapprochement owed much to the willingness of Kishida and Yoon to spend political capital. But it also reflected an awareness in both countries of the increased threat to security in East Asia from the Russia–Ukraine war. Kishida's linking of European and Asian security has already been noted. But South Korean strategic anxiety has also risen as the relationship between Moscow and Pyongyang has blossomed. In addition to the Russia–North Korea Treaty on Comprehensive Strategic Partnership, which pledged stronger cooperation in areas such as security, trade and cultural ties, North Korea has been shipping materiel to Russia for use in its war against Ukraine. Towards the end of 2024, North Korean troops entered combat alongside Russian forces in Russia's efforts to dislodge Ukrainian forces from the Russian territory of Kursk just over the border from Ukraine.[73] President Vladimir Putin also made a state visit to Pyongyang in mid-2024.[74]

The recognition of this strategic shift was reflected in the joint statement issued by then US president Joe Biden, Kishida and Yoon following the historic trilateral summit at Camp David in August 2023.[75] Of particular note was the statement's reference to 'our collective interests and security'. Japan and South Korea have hitherto eschewed recognising security links, reflecting factors including Japan's reluctance to commit to becoming itself directly involved in a conflict with North Korea, and lingering suspicions among some in South Korea of Japanese militarism. Indeed, the trilateral Camp David statement was the first recognition by Japan of the importance of

South Korea to Japan's security since the 'Korea clause' in the November 1969 communiqué between US president Richard Nixon and Japanese prime minister Sato Eisaku.[76] This recognition was made against a background of instability in Asia arising from the Vietnam War and the threat from a newly nuclear China.

Strategic imperative for both Japan and South Korea notwithstanding, the rapprochement remains fragile. Sceptics about its sustainability and even desirability exist in in both countries, and the United States' enthusiasm for supporting warmer Tokyo–Seoul relations may well weaken under the second Trump administration and indeed beyond. Moreover, South Korean domestic politics appear notably unstable following the domestic political crisis triggered by Yoon's failed attempt to declare martial law in late 2024. Left-wing South Korean parties are often more hostile to Japan; at the time of writing, it was unclear whether they might soon be back in power. Those supporting the rapprochement in Tokyo, Seoul and Washington will be hoping that the efforts made at the Camp David summit to institutionalise US–Japan–South Korea strategic cooperation through, for example, establishing trilateral 'annual, named, multi-domain trilateral exercises' help to at least maintain some momentum.[77]

The uncertainty over the trajectory of Japan–South Korea relations matters for Japan's grand strategy given that productive bilateral relations are a strategic amplifier for the US alliance network in Asia more broadly and thus for Japan's own security. A formal security alliance between Japan and South Korea is unlikely, reflecting the issues that have long stood in the way of a mutual acknowledgement of shared security concerns. But friction between the two also compromises the effectiveness of the United States' security relationship with each. This was evident in the threat by South Korea in 2019 to cancel bilateral intelligence-sharing under the 2016 General Security of Military Information Agreement (GSOMIA), which enables direct intelligence-sharing by Japan and South Korea. This matters for monitoring North Korea's missile tests. The US was alarmed at Seoul's threat, highlighting the need from Washington's point of view for Japan and South Korea to work together in the interests of regional security.[78]

Japan's deepening relations with NATO as one of the so-called Indo-Pacific Four (IP4), along with Australia, New Zealand and South Korea, is also illustrative of the broadening geographical scope of Japan's defence diplomacy since 2022. The attendance by Kishida at the June 2022 NATO summit in Madrid was the first such by a Japanese prime minister.[79] Kishida also attended the 2023 and 2024 NATO summits, with then NATO secretary general Jens Stoltenberg noting at the former that 'no partner is closer than Japan' and emphasising the need to boost cooperation in areas such as new technology, space and supply chains.[80] The attendance of the IP4 at the 2022, 2023 and 2024 summits also provided an important cross-brace to their own coordination in the Indo-Pacific.

Japan–NATO links are not new – Abe Shinzo was the first Japanese prime minister to address NATO's decision-making body, in January 2007.[81] Abe and Stoltenberg also agreed in 2017 that 'the security environments of Asia and Europe are closely linked', prefiguring Kishida's observation in 2022 that Ukraine today could be East Asia tomorrow.[82] While NATO recognises the strategic challenge from China, stronger ties are also not likely to result in a direct NATO response to a Taiwan contingency. Taiwan clearly lies outside the parameters of 'Europe or North America' set out in the North Atlantic Treaty's Article 5 on collective defence.[83] Any response to a Taiwan crisis from Europe would most likely come in the form of individual country rear-area support for a US-led effort.

Neither is it realistic to expect Japan to give direct military support to any future European war. Rather, closer Japan–NATO ties should be seen in the context of the global and multi-domain nature of the strategic challenge from China and others, and the need for like-minded countries to share intelligence and expertise where they can. China's recent growing strategic links with Russia underline the importance of this.

CHAPTER THREE

New tools of Japanese security

To achieve these objectives, Japan needs a strategy that integrates its national responses at a higher level by taking a panoramic view of the diverse dimensions of international relations as a whole, where confrontation and cooperation are intricately intertwined.[1]

**Japan, Cabinet Secretariat,
'National Security Strategy of Japan', December 2022**

[Economic security] is a speciality of the Japanese system.[2]

**Dr Tobias Lindner, Minister of State
at the Federal Foreign Office of Germany, 2023**

Japan's 'comprehensive national power'

In its National Security Strategy (NSS) published in late 2022, the Japanese government writes of the need to deploy the full spectrum of state power to achieve Japan's security objectives. The government defines this 'comprehensive national power' as 'including diplomatic, defense, economic, technological and intelligence capabilities'.[3] The formulation 'comprehensive national power' is mentioned no fewer than seven times in the text, underlining its importance within the new thinking on national security in Tokyo. The 2013 NSS, by contrast, mentioned Japan's 'national power' once and did not link the various channels of state power into a single presentation of Japanese power. This also dovetails with the focus in the new NSS on an 'integrated' approach to security strategy, reflecting the spillover of national security into previously separate areas such as the economy, and the need for Japan to break down the siloes – both governmental and societal – that stand in the way of the optimisation of Japanese security. The introduction of comprehensive national power into Japan's security discussion is also further evidence of the eclipse of the Yoshida Doctrine. Japan's deteriorating external environment means that the compartmentalisation of state power implicitly assumed in the Yoshida Doctrine no longer serves Japanese security interests. This also recognises the breadth of the challenge to Japan from China, which has had its own version of comprehensive national power since the 1990s.

The notion of comprehensive national power is not entirely new to Japan. In 1979, then-prime minister Ohira Masayoshi set up a study group on 'comprehensive security' (*Sōgo Anzenhoshō Kenkyū Gurūpu*) to consider Japanese security. This was one of nine study groups initiated by Ohira, which were designed to be advisory bodies for his administration as he sought policy advice from outside the narrow confines of Nagatacho (the location of the Diet in Tokyo).[4] Comprehensive security was a radical concept for its time in Japan, as it was the first time that Japan had included economic issues in its national-security thinking. These included threats to Japan's economic welfare such as interruptions to its energy supply and the need for Japan to take on a greater global role in terms of its economy as a 'member of the West'.[5] The study group on comprehensive security included experts, bureaucrats and others from a wide range of disciplines and ministries, evidence of the breadth of Ohira's definition of security.[6]

Ohira's death in office in 1980 stymied further development and implementation of the concept. His immediate successor as prime minister, Suzuki Zenko, set up a Ministerial Council on Comprehensive Security (*Sōgo Anzenhoshō Kakuryō Kaigi*) in 1980 to promote policies in this area, but the focus of deliberations moved to the non-military tools of security at the expense of Ohira's 'comprehensive' vision.[7] Suzuki's main policy focus also lay with fiscal and administrative reform against the background of Japan's deteriorating fiscal position.[8] His time in office was also relatively brief at just two years, further limiting scope for sustained policy change. Suzuki's successor, Nakasone Yasuhiro, meanwhile, switched Japanese strategy from the broad focus of Ohira to one of closer alignment with the United States.

There are echoes of Ohira's comprehensive security in the 2022 comprehensive national power concept. One such concerns the change in the relative balance of power arising from the decline of US economic vitality in the 1960s and 1970s.[9] But the context and drivers are different. For one thing, relations between Japan and China were good when Ohira was in office, and Tokyo saw Beijing as benign rather than as a threat. There were good reasons for this. Deng Xiaoping had, for example, paid a highly successful visit to Japan in 1978, during which he also lunched with the emperor, to sign the bilateral Treaty of Peace and Friendship and to seek inspiration from Japanese industry for his own reform programme in China, and in 1979 Ohira had initiated the programme of Japanese soft loans to China.[10] Ohira also strongly supported the deepening of Japanese relations with China and had played a key role in prime minister Tanaka Kakuei's push to normalise Sino-Japanese ties in 1972.

For another, Ohira's premiership coincided with Japan's transition from its years of rapid economic growth, which had lasted roughly from the 1950s until the first oil shock of 1973, to economic maturation and lower growth rates. As a former Ministry of Finance bureaucrat and finance minister, Ohira was also conscious of the precariousness of Japan's fiscal position against this background. As a result of the economic strains brought about by the 1973 oil shock, in 1975 Japan had, for example, started to issue large amounts of deficit-financing bonds for the first time since the end of the Second World War.[11] Fiscal reform was therefore one of Ohira's policy priorities when he came to power in 1979.

Thus, although Ohira's programme called for an increase in defence spending, he was also keen to deploy other means of state power for security to limit the speed of increases on defence.[12] US scholar of Japanese defence policy Richard Samuels has highlighted how Ohira's push for comprehensive national security was also informed by a need 'to justify low defence spending', 'emphasis[ing] Japan's commitments to diplomacy and to foreign economic policy' and 'divert[ing] attention away from anything having to do with things that go bang in the night'.[13] Moreover, in the US, both the Carter and the Reagan administrations viewed comprehensive security as a potential cover for Japanese mercantilism.[14] Samuels describes the 2022 NSS as an important rethinking of 'the concept of comprehensiveness' in Japan.[15] Indeed, combined with the plan to increase the defence budget noted elsewhere, rather than being a tool for fiscal restraint, Japan's comprehensive national power of 2022 is framed within the need to devote more national wealth to defence issues.

Japan's evolving geo-economic power

This *Adelphi* defines geo-economics as the interplay of a country's economic power with its foreign-policy aims. Japan's efforts to deploy its economic power credibly as an instrument of national security and foreign policy – what we might now call 'geo-economic power' – moved in fits and starts in the 1980s, 1990s and early 2000s. In part this was owing to economic friction with the US in the 1980s and early 1990s on the back of the large trade imbalance in Japan's favour, which forced Japan onto the policy defensive. Rather than strategically deploying its economic heft overseas, in this period Japan's policymakers were forced to placate the US, with, for example, Japan agreeing in 1986 to voluntary export constraints on semiconductors exported to the US and, astonishingly, to third countries, and promising to open its domestic market to imports.[16]

In his memoirs, George Shultz, US secretary of state in 1982–89 under president Ronald Reagan, describes the broader strategic concerns of those alarmed by Japan's economic rise: 'was Japan trying to achieve by sheer economic power what it wasn't able to achieve with military power?'.[17] In the event, Shultz need not have worried, as a large part of Japan's 'economic power' was channelled into a vast Japanese corporate shopping spree, driven by the currency windfall from the 1985 Plaza Accord agreement, which was designed to weaken the US dollar, strengthen the yen and the Deutschmark, and so boost US exports. Many of these acquisitions had to be sold again after the Japanese asset bubble burst in the early 1990s. Between 1989 and 1993, for example, the value of Japan's investments in the US alone fell by 50% to under US$15 billion on the back of these Japanese fire sales.[18] Japan's main strategic economic influence in this period largely derived from less politically controversial overseas development aid (ODA), which rose rapidly. By 1995, Japan had overtaken the US as the largest provider of ODA globally.[19]

Japan's efforts at building geo-economic institutions in this period also met headwinds. Japan was, along with Australia, one of the main agitators for the formation of the Asia-Pacific Economic Cooperation (APEC) forum in 1989.[20] Japan and others hoped that APEC would help to sustain the interest of the US, one of the founding members, in Asia as well as provide a forum for interaction between the US and China, which joined in 1991 along with Taiwan. But APEC momentum ebbed in the 1990s, owing to China's concerns that the forum could become a conduit for further increasing US influence in the region, as well as worries within Japan about the impact of trade liberalisation on its own key sectors.[21]

Additionally, in the 1990s, US Asia policy under president Bill Clinton was tilting back towards China, further complicating Japanese efforts to deploy geo-economic power. Clinton's focus on building relations with China during his two terms in office assumed that increased trade with it would ensure that it remained a benign global actor. Clinton believed that supporting China's accession to the World Trade Organization (WTO) would also mean that it would 'import one of democracy's most cherished values, economic freedom', and that this would democratise China.[22] For Tokyo, however, a US focus on China also meant what became known in Japan as 'Japan passing' in favour of China – literally so in 1998 when Clinton paid a nine-day visit to China without stopping in Tokyo. Clinton's own domestic political problems – not least the Democrats losing to the Republicans in both Houses of Congress in the 1994 midterm elections, the first time that this had happened since 1952 – also heralded a politically driven return to the berating of Japan by the Clinton administration for its closed markets. As the Asian financial crisis ripped through the region in 1997, Japanese efforts to bring about financial stabilisation through the creation of an Asian Monetary Fund (AMF) also foundered, largely on US concerns about the potential threat from an AMF to the US-led IMF.

Japan's ability to deploy credibly its economic influence as an instrument of national-security and foreign policy would have to wait until Abe Shinzo's second term as prime minister. Abe was successful in projecting Japan's geo-economic power for two main reasons. The first was his integrated view of policy to support Japanese grand strategy. Abe understood that effective projection of national power required a combination of internal and external balancing, that is, that Japan's national interests and security would be best served through a strengthened domestic economy and institutions as well as reinforcing Japan's existing external relationships and building new ones. A strengthened economy, to be delivered through his signature 'Abenomics' programme of economic reforms and supportive monetary and fiscal policy, would also serve to cement domestic public support for reforms elsewhere.[23] His failure to focus on pocketbook issues dear to voters had been one of the reasons for the failure of his short-lived first administration in 2006–07.

The speed with which Abe implemented major elements of this integrated policy agenda after regaining office in December 2012 was striking and underscored his programmatic approach to effecting change. Thus, in January 2013 he announced the details of his Abenomics programme; in December 2013 he published Japan's first NSS and established Japan's first National Security Council (NSC); in January 2014 he set up the NSC's coordinating body, the National Security Secretariat; and in July 2014 he initiated major security-related legislation that was presented to the Diet in May 2015 to enable that year's revision to the Guidelines for Japan–US Defense Cooperation.

The second reason for Abe's success at geo-economic power projection reflected changes in the international environment, which validated his world view. Abe was an early proselytiser for the importance of the rule of law. He wrote about this, for example, in 2006 in his book *Utsukushii Kuni E* (Towards a beautiful country), citing respect for the rule of law as a shared value between Japan and the US and other 'liberal nations of the world' (*sekai no jiyūshugi koku*).[24] His keynote speech to the IISS Shangri-La Dialogue in 2014 reflected this with its subtitle: 'Japan for the rule of law. Asia for the rule of law. And the rule of law for all of us.'[25] As noted in Chapter One, the Free and Open Indo-Pacific (FOIP) concept announced by Abe in 2016 was and remains at its heart a maritime framework, with international law essential to maintain openness and stability in the domain.

Abe recognised the threat to Japanese security from the efforts of China and others to disrupt the status quo, not just militarily but also through Beijing's exercising of its large geo-economic power. China's global Belt and Road Initiative (BRI) investment programme, launched in 2013, is one important example of the latter and, despite its problems, has been a major tool for the projection of Chinese influence around the world. As of this writing, Japan was one of only a handful of Asian countries that had not joined the BRI and is unlikely to do so. Japan also stands aside from other international organisations set up by Beijing that might threaten the current rules-based order. Thus, Tokyo has not joined the multilateral Asian Infrastructure Investment Bank (AIIB), which was officially launched in 2016, is headquartered in Beijing and, as its name indicates, provides investment for Asian infrastructure investment in the Asia region.

The intensification of Sino-US tensions, particularly since US President Donald Trump's first administration in 2017–21, increased economic and territorial menacing by China in pursuit of its geopolitical aims, as well as the flagrant breach of international law evident in Russia's invasion of Ukraine in 2022 have focused attention on the threat to global stability from the undermining of international law. The saving of the Trans-Pacific Partnership (TPP) mega trade bloc and its rebirth in 2018 as the Comprehensive and Progressive Agreement for Trans-Pacific Partnership (CPTPP) after Trump withdrew the US from the TPP in 2017 owed much to Abe's efforts. The CPTPP has since become an important strategic counterweight to the China-dominated Regional Comprehensive Economic Partnership (RCEP), which was launched in 2020, particularly in terms of the CPTPP's high standards and innovations in digital commerce. That in 2021 China also formally applied to join the CPTPP is surely a reflection of the bloc's strategic importance (see Figure 2).

Figure 2: **Asia's trade blocs**

Japan's deployment of geo-economic tools has evolved further since the start of Russia's war against Ukraine in 2022. It was, for example, a key player in the evolution of US-led economic state-craft since the Russian invasion, notably joining the sanctioning coalition that formed shortly afterwards and strengthening its sanctions in tandem with the other members of the G7.[26] Japan has also been a party to G7 efforts to use frozen Russian central-bank assets to raise funds for Ukraine's war effort.[27] While Japan has maintained its oil and liquefied-natural-gas projects on the Russian island of Sakhalin owing to the fragility of Japanese energy security, the long-term future of the projects looks uncertain. As seen in Chapter One, Japan's economic moves against Russia have come at the cost of already slim hopes of reaching an agreement with Moscow over the disputed Northern Territories/Southern Kuril Islands. But in so doing Japan has also underscored its role as a critical non-US/European voice within the G7 in upholding international law. This has become more important given China's courting of the so-called Global South through, for example, its BRI largesse.

Economic security – increasing Japanese geo-economic agency

Strong economic security, or the broad resilience of the national economy, is an essential pillar of a country's ability to project geo-economic power. This is particularly the case now that, as Russia's invasion of Ukraine has shown, economics and finance are also domains of conflict. Japan's reliance on imported resources for almost all its needs has long made it sensitive to threats to supplies of items needed for its economic growth and survival, such as hydrocarbons and food. The first oil shock of 1973 was a policy watershed in this regard. Indeed, changes made to energy efficiency, for example, in the years after 1973 meant that Japan was far better equipped to weather the second oil shock, which followed the 1979 Iranian Revolution, than were its rich-country peers.[28] As one scholar of Japanese economic history observes, economic security has been 'in the DNA of Japanese statecraft'.[29]

But, while Abe set about strengthening Japan's geo-economic power during his second administration, it was not until the latter stages of his second term in office that the changing demands of bolstering economic security received sustained government focus beyond the narrow confines of securing resources. Thus, for example, Abe focused on promoting open data flows in his 2019 Data Free Flow with Trust initiative on the sidelines of the G20 summit in Osaka to counter the fragmentation of global data flows as a result of data nationalism in China, Russia and elsewhere. Thus, too, an economics unit in the National Security Secretariat was established in April 2020, and in the same month Japan's Foreign Exchange and Foreign Trade Act was revised to lower from 10% to 1% of ownership the threshold above which regulatory approval was needed for an investment by a foreign entity in listed Japanese shares in sectors that might impact national security.[30]

Abe's successor but one as prime minister, Kishida Fumio, meanwhile, created the role of economic security minister in 2021 – the minister has cabinet rank and staff but does not have a ministry. As of early 2025, there had been three economic security ministers. The first two, Kobayashi Takayuki and Takaichi Sanae, both from the Liberal Democratic Party (LDP), were tasked with piloting specific economic-security measures through parliament. In the case of the former, this was the Economic Security Promotion Law, which was passed by the Diet in 2022 and dealt with supply-chain security, the security of core infrastructure, promoting public–private cooperation in technology, and patent non-disclosure.[31] In the case of the latter, this was the drawing up of a law to reinforce the Japanese security-clearance system to include economic security.[32] This was needed to strengthen Japan's own information security as well as to facilitate greater participation by Japanese individuals in international projects and thus strengthen Japan's domestic knowledge base.

Economic security and industrial policy

The institutional changes outlined above have helped to turn Japan into something of a pioneer in economic security. Moreover, the focus on economic security and, relatedly, on industrial policy by governments in the US and Europe has boosted Japan's geo-economic agency, enabling it to exploit its strengths in key technologies and hence its position in strategic supply chains. This has been particularly evident in the semiconductor sector. Predominance in this sector is now the focus of intense strategic competition between the US and China. Japan, despite the secular decline in its chip industry, retains strengths, and its semiconductor-manufacturing potential has attracted US interest as the latter seeks to bind its allies and partners more closely into its semiconductor supply-chain network to boost its own economic security.

Global attention on economic security has been accompanied by a refocus on industrial policy in the US, Europe and Japan. Under president Biden this brought the introduction in 2022 of major legislation such as the Inflation Reduction Act (IRA) and the CHIPS and Science Act (CHIPS Act), both of which were designed to reinforce US resilience and advantage in key areas of technology. This represents a significant shift from the framework that guided US policy from the 1980s until the deterioration of Sino-US relations in the latter part of the 2010s, which included reducing trade barriers, promoting inward foreign direct investment and lifting restrictions on market competition.

In some respects, this should work in Japan's favour, not least because of the tightening and reconfiguring of government–business relations required to implement economic-security policy successfully. Japan's post-war growth miracle was partly built on effective public–private strategic cooperation in economic development. Japanese government–business relations have, of course, changed since the high-water mark in the 1980s of what US political scientist Chalmers Johnson termed the Japanese 'developmental state' in his classic volume on the economic history of Japan, *MITI and the Japanese Miracle: The Growth of Industrial Policy, 1925–1975*.[33] One reason for this change was the rise in outward direct investment by Japanese firms from the 1980s, which diluted the influence over Japan's multinational companies of the then Ministry of International Trade and Industry (MITI, since renamed the Ministry of Economy, Trade and Industry). The market, administrative and political reforms of the 1990s and early 2000s – implemented in the wake of Japan's post-bubble asset-price crash, a series of scandals, some involving government–business ties, and the LDP's first fall from power in 1993 – further reduced the government's ability to control corporate Japan. That said, Japan's historical experience with industrial policy gives it an advantage over some of its G7 peers for whom this is a relatively new field.

Semiconductors have been one focus of recent Japanese industrial policy. In an effort to rebuild its semiconductor base, Japan's government has been aggressively deploying subsidies to promote domestic chip investments. This is part of Japan's strategy to achieve 'strategic autonomy' (*senryakuteki jiritsu-sei*) and 'strategic indispensability' (*senryakuteki fukaketsusei*), that is, a strengthening of strategic autonomy and identifying supply-chain choke points that Japan can dominate and so increase its resilience to and ability to deter foreign coercion.[34] The targets are ambitious: for example, by 2031, Tokyo hopes to raise its semiconductor wafer self-sufficiency rate to 44%, from 5% in 2022.[35] However, unlike Japanese industrial policy hitherto, which was directed towards domestic companies, the government is now prepared to subsidise foreign companies. The flagship of this new strategy so far has been the building of a semiconductor fabrication plant (fab) by Taiwan's TSMC, the world's largest chip maker, in Kikuyo in Kumamoto Prefecture on the southernmost main island of Kyushu. The fab was opened in early 2024 and makes chips of between 12 and 28 nanometres (nm), which have a wide range of applications, including cars and image sensors. This is an example of Japan's push to achieve strategic autonomy in technology critical to the functioning of the broad economy.[36] At this writing, TSMC was also planning to build a second fab in Kikuyo to produce 6 nm chips.[37] The government is funnelling some ¥1.2 trillion (US$7.9 bn) of state funds into the project.[38]

Notwithstanding teething issues with finding sufficient numbers of staff with the requisite skills, TSMC's presence in Kikuyo has had a significant beneficial economic impact both on the town itself and regionally in Kyushu, which the government hopes will allow it to recoup the cost to it of the subsidies extended.[39] These costs have included the provision of new infrastructure to support the growth in population associated with the current and future TSMC fab, and a linked rise in land prices.[40] Transport links between Taiwan and Kumamoto have also increased, while TSMC's presence has drawn in Japanese and other high-technology firms, turning Kyushu into a strategic-technology node for East Asia. The investment stake in the second TSMC plant announced by Japan's largest carmaker, Toyota Motor Corporation, in early 2024 was noteworthy given the strategic importance of the automotive sector to Japan's broader economic health.[41]

Japan's government has also committed substantial funding of nearly ¥1trn (US$6.7bn) to a second semiconductor project, that in Chitose on the northern island of Hokkaido (see Map 1, p. 8).[42] This enterprise is run by a start-up firm, Rapidus, which was set up in 2022 and is funded by eight large Japanese companies, including DENSO, Sony and Toyota. Some of the funding firms have also taken a stake in TSMC's Japanese venture. This is, however, a more experimental project than that of TSMC in Kikuyo and is designed to position Japan at the bleeding edge of chip technology – and thus achieve strategic indispensability – through Rapidus's collaboration with US technology firm IBM.

When completed in 2027, the Rapidus plant will mass-produce 2 nm chips, which will be used in advanced-technology areas such as artificial intelligence and quantum computing. However, no company has yet been able to produce 2 nm chips, with the result that demand prospects are unquantified. Moreover, despite Rapidus's collaboration with IBM, the project remains vulnerable to a potential future US desire to repatriate high-end technology. Future funding needs for the project to be realised are also high, with potential sources of cash as yet unidentified.[43] The funding shortfall may be as high as ¥4trn (US$26bn).[44] The government may therefore find itself assuming a greater share of the financial burden to sustain the project. If TSMC's Kikuyo project highlights the potential upsides of concerted industrial strategy for Japan, memories of the bankruptcy of Elpida Memory in 2012 point to the risks lurking in a market where demand and prices are prone to considerable volatility and fierce competition. When it failed, Elpida was the world's third-largest manufacturer of dynamic random-access memory (DRAM) chips for personal computers (and Japan's last remaining DRAM maker). The government had also invested funds in it to sustain its operations.[45]

CHAPTER FOUR

Structural impediments

If one does not understand what the rivalry is about, one is unlikely to have a secure intellectual grip on the subject of how best to prosecute it or to have anything worthy of respect to contribute on the issue of its prospective duration and the terms, if any, for its possible conclusion.[1]

Colin S. Gray, *The Geopolitics of Super Power*, 1988

To defend a country is an art, in fact, not a science. The challenge is that we can train scientists, but we cannot teach students to be artists. We can only educate them to appreciate art.[2]

Jakub Grygiel, 'Educating for National Security', 2013

Japan acquires its strategic 'rheostat'

The previous chapters of this *Adelphi* have attempted to illustrate the extent of the strategic change in Japan in recent years, particularly since the start of the current decade. Few if any countries have travelled the strategic distance that Japan has from the end of the Second World War until now – from demilitarisation and anti-militarism, to rapid rearming and preparation for great-power conflict. In his memoirs, which were published in the early 1990s, George Shultz argued that 'there is a feeling that [the Japanese] don't have a rheostat, only a switch that can go on or off but is difficult to moderate', and that the United States' role should be 'to provide the rheostat'.[3] It is hard to imagine a senior member of a US administration saying this today, despite the continued pressures from the US for Japan and other US allies to contribute more to regional and global stability. Indeed, given the likely continued focus on Sino-US competition in Washington, Japan is now probably the United States' most important ally. At the very least, without

Japanese logistical support, the US would struggle to contain contingencies on either the Korean Peninsula or Taiwan.

But two key questions remain. The first is whether these strategic changes are in themselves sufficient to meet the physical threat posed by the deterioration in Japan's external environment. The second is whether Japan is ready more broadly, particularly societally, to meet the challenges arising from this. The second question becomes more urgent if, as noted in the Introduction, any conflict in the region is protracted. As US historian Iskander Rehman notes in a recent *Adelphi* volume, 'neither the political nor the operational dimensions of the Sino-US security dynamic render a short, sharp war very likely'.[4] Indeed, persuading, say, Chinese President Xi Jinping that a protracted and resource-draining conflict over Taiwan is a more likely prospect than a quick victory for China should it invade the island is also a key element of the deterrence credibility of the US and its network of allies in the Indo-Pacific region.

At the core of Japanese national-security policy lie two priorities. The first is to build Japanese deterrence and response capability, and the second is to reinforce economic and societal resilience. Japan is acquitting itself relatively well regarding what may be seen as the four main pillars of a successful deterrence strategy: political will, military capability, coalition credibility, and messaging or clarity of narrative.[5] Notwithstanding their lack of combat experience since 1945, Japan's armed forces boast a formidable array of equipment, including, as described in earlier chapters, nascent force-projection capabilities. Albeit officially framed within Japan's constitutional and normative constraints, the lethality of Japan's armed forces is also rising. The building up of the credibility of Japan's military forces in recent years has been 'incremental but nevertheless relentless'.[6] Japan is

Figure 3: **Japanese and Chinese GDP compared, 1960–2023**

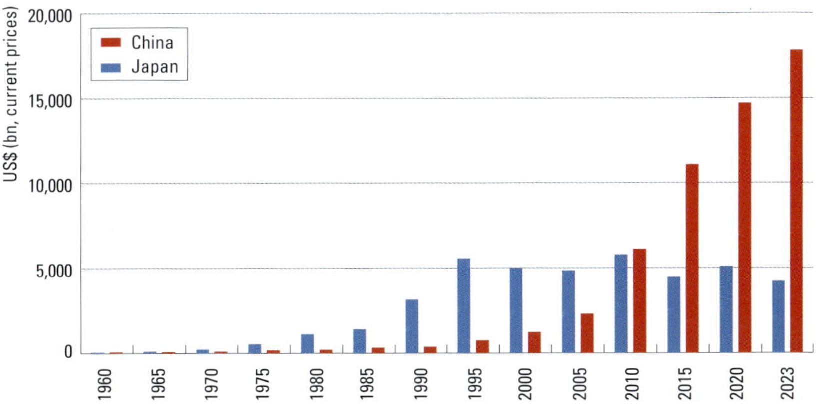

Source: World Bank   ©IISS

thus steadily reinforcing the 'threat' or 'offensive' component needed for any credible deterrence and response strategy. With the new concept of 'comprehensive national power', it is also now explicitly deploying more of its national power towards its national-security goals. Its recognition of the importance of developing its technology base and intelligence capabilities in building its deterrence and response credibility is one key element of this.

In doing so Japan has also increased its value within the US–Japan security alliance. In the 1990s and up to the early 2000s, Japan, like others, underestimated both the speed and impact on Asia's balance of power of China's rise. In 1990, China's GDP was just over one-tenth the size of Japan's (in current US$ terms).[7] By 2010, China had overtaken Japan, and by 2020 its economy was nearly three times as big (see Figure 3).[8] Increases in China's defence budget have been similarly dizzying: in 2000, China's and Japan's defence budgets were similar in size, but by 2020 China's defence spending was four times that of Japan, and the gap has widened since (see Figure 1, p. 18).[9]

For Japan, increasing integration within the US security alliance thus makes strategic sense. Given the asymmetry of size so significantly in China's favour, China has little to fear from Japan on its own.

The threat to Japanese security from China, North Korea and, recently, Russia has forced Japan to increase the potency of its defence capabilities. The Japanese government describes its focus as being 'on the capabilities of [Japan's] opponents and new ways of warfare'.[10] This contrasts with the previous posture of maintaining only the minimum necessary defence force that could be scaled up should the situation require.[11] While this allowed Japan to keep defence spending low and to allay the then-still-strong fears of a revival of Japanese militarism in the region, it was also a posture that in effect assumed no adversaries. Such an approach is clearly no longer fit for purpose given the accumulation of security risks to Japan in East Asia. The new posture, by contrast, thus rightly calls for readiness to meet specific threats to Japan's security and survival. Targets for delivery of the 2022 National Security Strategy (NSS) in terms of timelines and funds also underscore the seriousness of Japan's strategic change, reinforcing the strategic messaging from Tokyo.

It is also important to acknowledge that Japan has untapped military power. Japan is, for example, one of a handful of countries that are latent nuclear powers, that is, they have the technological ability to develop nuclear weapons of their own. (In Asia, this group also includes South Korea and Taiwan.) Japan's large and sophisticated industrial base features advanced nuclear technologies, including uranium enrichment and plutonium reprocessing. Estimates of how long it would take Japan to produce a nuclear weapon range from around six months, as is suggested 'in Western circles', to three to five years, with one to two years possible in a crisis situation.[12]

Japan's active space programme adds the possibility of delivery capability to this nuclear latency.

Some Japanese politicians have advocated the acquisition of nuclear weapons, particularly given the concerns about the threat to Japan from Chinese and North Korean nuclear weapons.[13] In a variation on this theme, in 2022, after leaving office as prime minister, Abe Shinzo argued that Japan should discuss 'nuclear sharing' as is practised in NATO, in which countries in the bloc host US nuclear weapons but are allowed to have a voice in deciding on their use.[14] Abe's suggested démarche was, however, quickly shut down by then-prime minister Kishida Fumio, one of whose policy platforms was the bringing about of 'a world without nuclear weapons'.[15]

Views such as Abe's remain a minority, given the moral aversion to nuclear weapons among the Japanese public as a result of Japan's unique status as the only country to have suffered a nuclear attack. Japan's status as a signatory to the Nuclear Non-Proliferation Treaty (NPT) also militates against change in the near term. In Japan, much will depend, however, on the credibility of the United States' extended deterrence, which, as the second Trump administration starts, looks less certain than it has for many years. This also applies to South Korea, where concerns about US reliability in the face of North Korea's continued nuclear-weapons development have helped to stoke support in the country for an indigenous nuclear capacity.[16]

An erosion of US credibility or even the acquisition of nuclear capability by South Korea could prompt a rethink in Tokyo. One sign of change here might be reconsideration of the Three Non-Nuclear Principles (*Hikaku San Gensoku*). Announced to the Diet by prime minister Sato Eisaku in 1967 against a background of what Japan assumed was an easing of external threats, and adopted in 1968 by the Diet, these hold that Japan will not possess or make nuclear weapons or permit their introduction into Japanese territory.[17] In adopting these principles, Sato was in effect also committing Japan to relying on the US nuclear umbrella for its security.

Demographic and fiscal headwinds

There remain, however, three significant structural impediments relating to economic and societal resilience that overshadow Japan's broader strategic aims. The first is Japan's adverse demographic trajectory. In this Japan is not unique in Asia. In China, for example, the labour force started to shrink from 2016 and its population fell for the second year running in 2023.[18] South Korea's government has spent some US$270 billion since 2006 on pro-natalist policies to boost its flagging birth rate, but without success – the country's fertility rate is now below one birth per woman, less than half the replacement rate of just over two births and below even Japan's.[19] But Japan currently leads both China and South Korea for the intensity of its demographic change. Japan's working-age population has been falling since 1996, while the population aged 65 or over continues to rise, likely hitting 30% of the total towards the end of the 2020s. The number of births also continues to fall, dropping below 800,000 in 2022 for the first time since records began.[20] As a result of these trends, Japan's population has been declining each year since its 2009 peak. With a decline of 800,000 in 2022 and 860,000 in 2023, Japan's population is in effect losing the equivalent of the population of a medium-to-large city each year (see Figure 4).[21]

This has major implications for the staffing of Japan's armed forces at a time when the need for people with special skills has never been higher in its post-war history. As a report compiled for a Japanese Ministry of Defense (JMOD) expert panel in 2023 indicated, even with advanced equipment, Japan will be unable to demonstrate its defence capabilities without adequate

Figure 4: **Japan's demographic trends, 1935–2023**

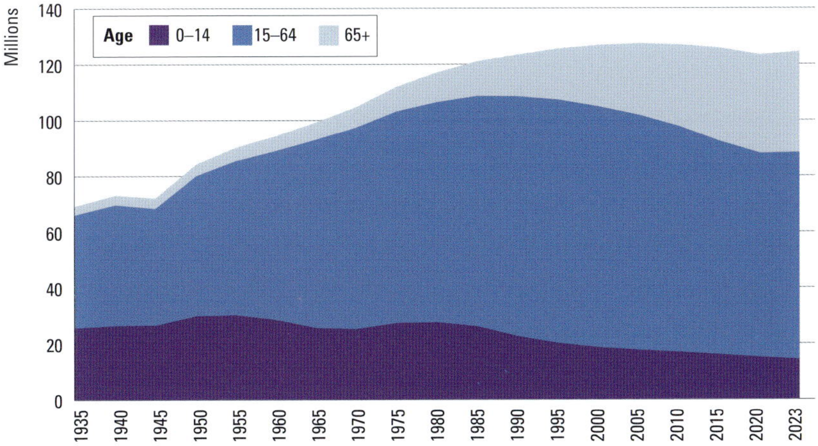

Source: Statistics Bureau of Japan, *Japan Statistical Yearbook*, various years   ©IISS

staffing levels.[22] Data from the JMOD suggests that the Self-Defense Forces (SDF) are already understaffed by just under 20,000, breaking down by main category to 13,000 for the Ground Self-Defense Force (GSDF), 2,000 for the Marine Self-Defense Force (MSDF) and 3,000 for the Air Self-Defense Force (ASDF).[23] Although the public standing of the SDF and indeed of the US–Japan alliance rose significantly as a result of the bilateral *Operation Tomodachi* disaster-relief efforts that followed the 2011 Tohoku earthquake and tsunami, recruitment remains a challenge.[24] JMOD data shows that in fiscal year 2023–24, for example, the SDF was only able to recruit 50.8% of its target for the year.[25] Competition from the private sector, where pay is higher and conditions less arduous, for Japan's dwindling cohort of youngsters is one key reason for this. The government plans to deploy technology to automate tasks where possible to offset this shortfall, but the impact of this personnel shortage on Japan's ability to expand its capabilities will remain severe. Increasing Japan's fleet of submarines, for example, to cope with the demands of a potential Taiwan contingency in Japan's southwestern region would require the MSDF to find an extra 70 people per submarine, a tall order given the current demographic trajectory.[26]

The second headwind relates to Japan's ability to support the drain on its fiscal resources for its defence reforms. As noted in the Introduction, Tokyo plans to boost Japanese defence spending to 2% of current-price GDP, or ¥43 trillion (US$300bn) by fiscal year 2027–28. Progress to date is good. The JMOD is planning for an over 7% year-on-year increase in defence spending in 2025–26 to ¥8.5trn (US$56bn), which would take the budget to 1.6% of GDP.[27] Other than interest payments on Japanese government bonds (JGBs), defence is now the fastest-rising major spending category in the central government's budget.[28] Notwithstanding that some of the increase will be achieved by re-categorising some existing spending, achieving the target and then sustaining it will require further hefty budget rises. Moreover, given the scale of the challenge to Japanese national security, the 2%-of-GDP target should probably also be seen as a long-term floor for defence spending rather than a ceiling, particularly with likely continued pressure from the US for its allies to contribute more to their own defence.

The defence-spending target also draws an important philosophical line under Japan's self-imposed limit of 1% of GNP/GDP. This had been put in place for domestic political purposes in 1976 by the administration of prime minister Miki Takeo, a noted defence dove. The international backdrop at the time of detente and a difficult domestic economic environment were political enablers for Miki's policy. Although prime minister Nakasone Yasuhiro had tried to push for higher Japanese defence spending, and in 1987 abolished the ceiling, he was only able to nudge spending above the limit by a small amount. Defence spending fell back under 1% of GNP after he left office.[29]

As with its demographic headwinds, Japan is not alone in facing fiscal constraints. Several European members of NATO, for example, are struggling to raise their defence spending to the NATO guideline of 2% of GDP.[30] But none has a fiscal profile like Japan's. IMF data shows that Japan's gross general government debt stock stood at an estimated 255% of GDP in 2024, or more than double the size of the economy. This reflects the economic adjustment and the subsequent prolonged period of deflation after the bursting of the economic bubble in the early 1990s. Particularly pernicious were the years of price deflation that set in during the late 1990s, which crimped nominal GDP while JGB issuance continued at a high level. In the nearly 20 years to 2024, Japan's general government debt doubled as a percentage of the economy.[31] This represents a weaker fiscal profile even than Italy, which has the most fragile public finances in the G7 – in 2024, the IMF estimated Italy's gross general government debt stock at just under 140% of GDP.[32] At an estimated 158% of GDP in 2024, Japan's net public-debt position is more favourable by dint of the significant assets held by the government, but this has also deteriorated significantly since the late 1990s and compares with the average that the IMF calculates for other advanced economies of just over 80%.[33]

Yet Japan's fiscal position is more stable than the overall ratios suggest, and a full-blown fiscal crisis is thus unlikely. This is owing to the high proportion of the JGB market held by domestic investors. At this writing, the Bank of Japan (the central bank) alone held just over 50% of JGBs outstanding as a result of the years of quantitative easing, and Japanese banks and insurance companies held another 30% or so of the market. Foreign investors, meanwhile, held less than 10% of outstanding JGBs. Given their sizeable holdings of government bonds, none of the local investors has an interest in destabilising the market.[34] With a tax take of around 34% of GDP, Japan is also undertaxed by the standards of many of its developed-country peers.[35] Japan thus has room to raise taxes in order to improve its fiscal position, although as a number of Japanese prime ministers have found to their cost, this carries with it considerable political risk. Another option might be to sell government-owned assets.

It is possible that pressures to ensure that Japan's grand strategy succeeds will trigger a fresh round of structural reforms that raise productivity and thus economic growth. But absent these, the structural pressures on Japan's fiscal position will only grow. A combination of the adverse demographic trends already described, particularly the ageing of society, and low overall economic growth will ensure competition for scarce public resources for defence spending from areas such as social security. The latter already accounts for one-third of total spending in 2024–25, up from 30% of the total in, for example, the draft budget for fiscal year 2010–11 and 20% for 2000–01.[36] Against this background, the public debate on how to prioritise resource allocation in the years to come is likely to be tough. Educating the public on the resource trade-offs needed to increase defence spending by the sums suggested will thus be critical for the success of the reforms. Rising concerns among the Japanese public about the threat from China may be a tailwind for this.

Societal change

Related to this is the third headwind, which concerns societal change and the interplay with the need to reinforce Japanese strategic culture. One legacy of Japan's distinctive post-war settlement is the marked gap between civil society on the one hand and the armed forces on the other. This reflected the strong anti-militarism of the left wing of Japan's political spectrum and the legacy of the Yoshida Doctrine pragmatists on the centre-right. Although Japan has only had two socialist prime ministers since the end of the Second World War and the Japanese Communist Party has never been in government, Japan's left wing was until the 1990s vigorous, taking strongly pro-pacifist and anti-constitutional-reform positions on national-security policy.[37] The Japanese political left and centre-left wing has also been broadly successful in its main goal of securing at least 30% of the seats in the Diet to prevent the Liberal Democratic Party (LDP) from making formal changes to the constitution – which stipulates that amendments can be initiated through concurring votes of two-thirds of all the members of each House, followed by a national referendum. Even though the LDP–Komeito coalition held super-majorities for part of Abe's second term, Abe did not move to change the constitution formally.

As in other countries, support for the left wing in Japan has been strong in education and academia, which were also a focus of US-led reform efforts during the 1945–52 occupation.[38] This was complemented by an effort to restore societal balance on the political centre-right after the large-scale protests that had accompanied LDP prime minister Kishi Nobusuke's pushing through the Diet of revisions to the US–Japan security treaty in 1960. Kishi's successor as LDP prime minister, Ikeda Hayato, sought to maintain domestic political stability by focusing on Japan's economic development, which he did for example through his 'income doubling' pledge, and deprioritising sensitive national-security and constitutional-change issues.

Thus was born the reluctance on the part of the Japanese research community to engage with military-related research on the one hand, and the low profile of Japan's defence-industrial sector on the other. The former was evident as recently as 2017 in the Science Council of Japan's (SCJ) restatement of its 1950 and 1967 position that the SCJ 'will never become engaged in scientific research for military purposes'.[39] The latter is seen in the relatively small roles defence operations play in Japan's largest conglomerates, with only weak synergies between defence arms and other operations of these groups.[40] Profit margins at Japan's defence contractors have traditionally been low, at around 8%, although, as part of its plans to strengthen Japan's defence-industrial base, the government would like to raise this to 15%.[41] Uninspiring financial performance in the sector has partly reflected its lack of exposure to foreign competition because of constraints on exports and the dominance of the JMOD as the main customer.

In addition to headline defence reforms already described, the 2022 NSS and National Defense Strategy (NDS) seek to narrow the civilian–military split in Japanese society. China's military–civil fusion policy, pursued under President Xi to modernise and strengthen China's armed forces, and North Korea's mobilisation of all its national resources in pursuit of its nuclear-weapons development have forced Japan's policymakers to confront this issue.[42] The NSS, for example, refers to the need for Japan to capitalise on its 'advanced technological capabilities' developed 'in the public and private sectors in the field of national security, without being bound by its conventional way of thinking'.[43] It also calls for the government and the private sector to work together in economic security as well as for Japan's public and private sectors to leverage advanced technological research for defence purposes.[44] In order to build public support for the changes being advocated, the NSS also recognises the need to work with local governments to 'develop [Japan's] defense architecture as a whole'.[45] This reflects the central government's need to build public support for increased military build-up in areas where this has traditionally been controversial (such as Okinawa, which hosts a large US military presence) as well as for associated changes in areas such as infrastructure resilience.

Japanese public opinion is changing. The lack of public protests following the release of the 2022 national-security documents was striking given the historic changes they contained. This contrasted with the national public outcry in 2015 at the legal changes to allow the SDF to engage in collective self-defence missions. Public-opinion polls also suggest a majority, albeit still a narrow one, in favour of the reforms. Concerns remain, however, over how increased spending on defence will be funded, with tax rises generally unpopular.[46] One driver of this change in opinion is increased public pessimism over Japan's own security. One poll taken in early 2024 found that over 80% of those surveyed thought that Japan's security was threatened.[47] Japanese public opinion towards China has also darkened, with over 90% of those surveyed in a 2023 poll expressing an 'unfavourable' or 'relatively unfavourable' view of China.[48] This, coupled with the electoral decline of Japan's left-wing parties and generational change, which has blunted left–right ideological friction over defence issues, is a tailwind for the government's wish to integrate Japan's civilian and military sectors.[49] But the government has set itself an ambitious task. If successful, this push for civilian–military integration will have a transformational impact on Japanese society. In many ways, therefore, this is as important an aspect of the 2022 national-security documents as the higher-profile requests such as those for equipment and capability upgrades.

As Japanese public opinion catches up with the country's changing security needs, so Japanese strategic culture risks falling behind Japan's defence-policy revolution. Each country's strategic culture is different, reflecting a range of factors including culture, history and geography. Colin Gray, for example, writing in the early 1980s, describes US 'strategic style' as '"managerial" rather than "strategic"', with a tendency to 'devote far more attention to the management of large defense programs than to operational issues'.[50] He notes too how this contributed to the United States' failure to understand the Soviet Union.[51]

Conversations that this author has had with former senior members of the United Kingdom government pointed to the UK's strategic style as 'globalised', and characterised by a strong drive for identifying 'business interests', 'belonging' to global institutions, and an ability to course correct when needed. These are all reflections of the historic primacy of the maritime domain in UK strategic thinking.

The comparison between Japan and the UK, two island middle powers sitting on either side of the Eurasian landmass, is illustrative. Kosaka Masataka contrasted what he viewed as a more outward-looking UK, which he described as a 'maritime nation' (*kaiyō koku*), with the more inward-looking 'island nation' (*shima guni*) of Japan, urging Japan to become more like the UK.[52] This *Adelphi* has argued that Japan has indeed become more externally focused as its external environment has become more threatening. Japanese policymakers have an acute grasp of the challenges to Japan's survival that these risks present. One observer has described Japan as having a 'panoramic threat perception' that has, certainly until Russia's full-scale invasion of Ukraine in 2022, been missing elsewhere in the political West.[53] Proximity to China has given Japan insights into what Australian international-relations scholar Coral Bell described as China's geopolitical 'tenacity' that Japan's partners would be well advised to study.[54] Given the importance of Japan now as a bulwark to support the stability of East Asia, this is to be welcomed. But Japan remains constrained by its post-Second World War norms inhibiting the development of a strategic culture that could be more fully supportive of the decisions that Japan may have to make in the lead-up to or the fighting in any conflict in its neighbourhood.

Most importantly, Japan lacks a buoyant security-studies base for the study of war. The US and the UK both have this foundation, which is also essential for understanding how, for example, war works, or how preparing for war and preparing to fight might differ. This owes much to the post-Second World War anti-militarism in some sectors of the academic and research communities noted elsewhere in this book. This is not to say that Japan's expert community does not examine conflict per se. But the preference is to filter conflict analysis through international relations, geopolitics and, more recently, geo-economics. An increasing number of think tanks are also focusing on these areas as Japan seeks to understand how to respond to the deterioration in its external environment. The important difference between international relations and geopolitics on the one hand and war studies on the other, however, is that while the former allows research to focus on others, the latter requires study of one's own country, that is, of wars won and lost. For Japan the latter remains difficult given the lingering political legacy of the Second World War and its immediate aftermath.

The setting up, for example, of defence-studies institutes in Japanese universities and elsewhere and their linking up with foreign peers would yield significant dividends in nurturing future Japanese strategic thinkers. The geopolitical trends in Japan's neighbourhood suggest that the demand for these will only grow. Creation of an effective strategic intellectual infrastructure in Japan could also contribute to the narrowing of Japan's civil–military gap via a more effective transmission of the issues at play into the public domain. This matters for preparing Japanese public opinion for further policy changes and the associated trade-offs that are likely to be necessary, as well as strategically. Japanese defence-policy scholar Mori Satoru describes public opinion as 'the centre of gravity' in any US–Japan–Taiwan resistance to Chinese aggression.[55] British historian Sir Michael Howard, meanwhile, cited 'public opinion' as one of the four 'tools' for a country's grand strategy in addition to 'armed force, wealth, and allies'.[56] Japan's public needs at the very least to be able to understand the consequences of the strategic choices that the government is making.

CONCLUSION

*War [had become] unthinkable but not impossible, and therefore
we must think about it.*[1]

Bernard Brodie, quoted in Zachary Jonathan Jacobson,
***On Nixon's Madness: An Emotional History*, 2023**

This *Adelphi* book has sought to place Japan's new grand
strategy within the context of its strategic journey since the
Meiji Restoration of 1868 in order to illuminate the ruptures
and continuities evident in it since Abe Shinzo's decisive
second administration of 2012–20. Abe played a key enabling
role in the evolution of Japanese grand strategy, laying its intellectual and institutional foundations. This centred on his early
appreciation of the looming challenge to both Japanese security
and the regional order from China's political, economic and
military rise, and on his understanding of the need for Japan
to integrate the various channels of state power to ensure its
security. While Abe made considerable progress in achieving
his aims, it was under the premiership of Kishida Fumio that
Abe's grand strategy achieved a credible military underpinning. This found expression in the security reforms laid out in
Japan's historic 2022 national-security documents.

This book has also sought to assess the effectiveness of this
evolution in Japan's grand strategy against the background of
what the Japanese government views as the most challenging
global security environment for the country since the end of

the Second World War. Concerns in Tokyo that China might seek to absorb Taiwan by force, and about the threat to Japan from strategic cooperation between China, Russia and North Korea, lie behind Tokyo's assessment. China, Russia, North Korea and Taiwan are all near or fairly close neighbours of Japan and either already or potentially hostile to it. It is therefore not surprising that Japan feels so strategically exposed.

Structural change in Japan

In its 2022 defence reforms Japan set itself an ambitious range of goals to ensure both its national security and, relatedly, the stability of the Indo-Pacific. Geopolitical changes in the region and the resulting threats to Japanese security have made achieving these goals and then ensuring that Japan's strategic posture keeps up with continued changes in its external environment urgent for Japan, its ally the United States and like-minded partners. Those concerned that Japan might slip back into its post-war Yoshida Doctrine comfort zone ignore the extent of the institutional, policy and societal changes that Japan has undergone, particularly since 2010.

These changes are often underappreciated. As described in the previous chapter, Japanese public opinion is now highly attuned to the risk to Japanese security from China. Moreover, Japan's post-war political divisions between left and right, with the left wing favourably disposed towards Beijing and antagonistic towards the US security alliance, have faded. Generational change has undercut support for the political left in Japan. This is not to say that Japanese public opinion is becoming actively belligerent, but rather that public expectations of how government policy is calibrated with regard to ensuring Japanese security have changed.

This change in public opinion also suggests continued support from across most of Japan's political spectrum for maintaining the US as the cornerstone of Japanese grand strategy. The left-leaning Democratic Party of Japan (DPJ), which took power from the Liberal Democratic Party (LDP) in a landslide victory in 2009, attempted to achieve equidistance from the US and China under the first of its three prime ministers, Hatoyama Yukio. His plan, outlined in 2009, for an East Asian Community, in which Japan would help to lead collective regional efforts to promote security and prosperity, and which in turn would help Japan to rebalance its relations with the US, is unlikely to be repeated.[2] The region's geopolitical backdrop has changed considerably in the past 15 years, and, despite public ire at recent LDP funding scandals and the party's management of the economy, memories of the DPJ's troubled record in government in 2009–12 remain fresh. Although the LDP–Komeito coalition performed poorly in the 2024 lower-house election, which produced Japan's first minority government since prime minister Hata Tsutomu's 64-day administration in 1994, the DPJ's successor party, the Constitutional Democratic Party (CDP), only increased its proportional-representation vote tally by 0.6% from the 2021 general election.[3]

But understanding the challenges to one's national security and being prepared to fight to defend it are, of course, not the same. This is particularly the case for a democracy such as Japan. Japan's plans to invest large sums in new military equipment and technology for new domains of defence such as space and cyber make strategic sense. The new national-security strategy has a five-year target for raising defence spending to 2% of GDP, but the increases will need to be sustained well beyond 2027 as Japan builds on its already formidable array of military hardware. Indeed, circumstances may dictate that 2% of GDP needs to be viewed as a spending floor rather than just a target. Yet Japan's military has not engaged in combat since the end of the Second World War, and there are questions over the willingness of Japanese young-sters to step forward should the need for a military response arise in the event, say, of a Taiwan contingency. A 2024 poll suggested that less than 10% of Japan's population would be prepared to fight for their country, one of the lowest rates globally.[4]

Japan is not alone in facing either of these challenges. China's armed forces, for example, have not seen active combat since its invasion of Vietnam in 1979, and a poll published in early 2024, for example, suggested that 38% of those aged under 40 would refuse to serve in the United Kingdom armed forces in the event of a new world war.[5] Japan's ageing and declining population further aggravates this problem, with the Japan Self-Defense Forces (SDF) regularly missing their recruitment targets. But this highlights the need for the Japanese government to famil-iarise public opinion further with the strategic challenges to Japanese security and the implications of the policy changes needed to meet them. The changes in Japanese public opinion over the past decade or so are remarkable given the decades-long primacy of the Yoshida Doctrine. There thus is no reason why further moves in public opinion are not possible.

The issue of change to Japan's constitutional constraints is often cited as an inhibitor of its ability to implement an effec-tive grand strategy. That even Abe, who for much of his second term was one of the most powerful of Japan's post-war prime ministers, felt unable to bring about the formal changes to the constitution that he had championed indicates how high the political barriers to revision remain in Japan. Although polls suggest that there is narrow majority support for revising the second paragraph of Article 9, which prohibits Japan from maintaining armed forces, the majority in favour of keeping the war-renouncing first paragraph of Article 9 remains hefty.[6] Japan's government has, however, long taken a pragmatic approach to the constitution, reinterpreting it where needed.

Its decision to regard the SDF (and its predecessors the Japanese National Safety Forces and then the National Police Reserve) as 'constitutional' at its founding in 1954 and Abe's 2014 reinterpretation are two examples. This evidenced pragmatism around interpretation of the constitution thus allows considerable leeway for further policy changes that Japan might need.

Japan's capacity to deliver

Japan is often criticised for its slow pace of change, whether economic, institutional or strategic. This has given rise to scepticism in some quarters as to whether Tokyo can deliver on its ambitious grand strategy. But this criticism is sometimes overdone. The rapidity of the transformative institutional reforms initiated at the start of the second Abe administration would have been impressive by the standards of any of Japan's G7 peers, for example. Even in the early 1990s to the early 2000s, the so-called 'lost decade' during which Japan was dealing with the legacy of the bursting of its economic bubble, it was able to implement far-reaching political and institutional reforms that 'strong' prime ministers such as Koizumi Junichiro and Abe used to advance their agendas. The change to Japan's electoral system (enacted in 1994 and implemented in the general election of 1996) and the overhauling of central government (enacted in 1999 and implemented in 2001) are two important examples of this.

As with most countries, substantial change in Japan has often come in response to crises or turning points. For Japan these have included the Meiji Restoration, defeat in the Second World War and, most recently, the increasing security threat from China. This *Adelphi* book has argued that Japan's evolving grand strategy is underpinned by a realistic appraisal of China as an actor in the region and beyond. Indeed, Japan's historic and cultural links with its neighbour give it a strategic understanding of China that could act as a force multiplier for its US ally and other partners. This book opened with a quotation from the 2022 National Security Strategy outlining the view of Japan's government on the danger presented to Japan's security by the deterioration in its external environment. It is therefore clear that Japan understands its strategic predicament and the drivers of it.

But enabling this grand strategy to succeed at all will require more significant change across Japanese society that will further challenge long-standing domestic norms and assumptions about the provision of national security. Japan also faces challenges in matching constrained domestic resources to its expanding national-security objectives. These are ambitious demands. But, as was outlined in Chapter One, Japan's experience with the Meiji Restoration shows that the country has been capable of initiating profound change across society when external conditions require. Indeed, British military historian John Keegan has described the Meiji Restoration as 'one of the most radical changes of national policy recorded in history'.[7] This *Adelphi* book has argued that the security challenge now facing Japan in effect demands a transformation of a similar range. Abe's second administration and the defence reforms initiated by the Kishida administration in 2022 have provided a solid foundation for an effective grand strategy, but the challenge now will be in integrating this with enabling 'software', whether this be economic or societal. Achieving this is essential to Japan's ability to meet the challenge from China and also to navigate its strategic relationship with its US ally.

NOTES

Introduction

1   Japan, Cabinet Secretariat, 'National Security Strategy of Japan', December 2022, p. 2, https://www.cas.go.jp/jp/siryou/221216anzenhoshou/nss-e.pdf.

2   For an excellent summary of what 'grand strategy' is and an explanation of the difference between 'grand strategy' and 'strategy', see Joshua Rovner, *Strategy and Grand Strategy* (Abingdon: Routledge for the IISS, 2025), for example, pp. 11–13.

3   Japan, Prime Minister's Office, 'The Constitution of Japan', 3 November 1946, https://japan.kantei.go.jp/constitution_and_government_of_japan/constitution_e.html#:~:text=Aspiring%20sincerely%20to%20an%20international,means%20of%20settling%20international%20disputes. Article 9 of the constitution also pledges that 'land, sea, and air forces, as well as other war potential, will never be maintained'.

4   The term 'Yoshida Doctrine' was coined by Professor Nishihara Masashi, a specialist in Japanese security studies and, from 1987 to 1994, a member of the IISS's Advisory Council.

5   For further details on the Yoshida Doctrine, see Yuka Koshino and Robert Ward, *Japan's Effectiveness as a Geo-economic Actor: Navigating Great-power Competition*, Adelphi 481–483 (Abingdon: Routledge for the IISS, 2022), pp. 19–20. 'Low posture' (*tei shisei*) was a term associated with Ikeda Hayato, prime minister in 1960–64. With his 'income-doubling' policy, Ikeda was also the architect of Japan's high-growth period.

6   See, for example, Yoshida Shigeru, *Kaisō Jū Nen* (Shinsho Ban) [Ten years' reminiscence] (Tokyo: Mainichi Wanz, 2022), p. 148.

7   Tanaka Akihiko, *Anzen Hoshō, Sengo 50 Nen no Mosaku* [Security: an exploration 50 years after the end of the war] (Tokyo: Yomiuri Shimbunsha, 1997), p. 146. See also J.W. Dower, *Empire and Aftermath: Yoshida Shigeru and the Japanese Experience 1878–1954* (Cambridge, MA and London: Harvard University Press, 1988), pp. 436–70,

for a discussion of the SDF's origins in the creation of the police force and the accompanying political and constitutional debates.

8   The Soviet Union did not sign the Treaty of San Francisco, however. This reflected, inter alia, Soviet disapproval of the linking of the treaty to the US–Japan security agreement.

9   Sakamoto Kazuya, *The Bonds of the Japan–US Alliance: The Japan–US Security Treaty and the Search for Mutuality* (Tokyo: Japan Publishing Industry Foundation for Culture, 2022), p. 264.

10   Zbigniew Brzezinski, *The Grand Chessboard: American Primacy and Its Geostrategic Imperatives* (New York: Basic Books, 1998), p. 173.

11   Aono Toshihiko, *Reisenshi, Betonamu Senso Kara Soren Hōkai Made* [History of the Cold War from the Vietnam War to the fall of the Soviet Union] (Tokyo: Chuo Koron Shinsha, 2023), p. 160.

12   Keith Bradsher, 'Amid Tension, China Blocks Vital Exports to Japan', *New York Times*, 22 September 2010, https://www.nytimes.com/2010/09/23/business/global/23rare.html.

13   For more detail on the defence changes ushered in by Nakasone, Koizumi and Abe, see Robert Ward, 'Another Special Relationship? The United States and Japan', *Survival: Global Politics and Strategy*, vol. 66, no. 3, June–July 2024, pp. 205–6. See also Japan, Ministry of Foreign Affairs, 'The Guidelines for Japan–U.S. Defense Cooperation', 27 April 2015, https://www.mofa.go.jp/files/000078188.pdf.

14   The National Defense Strategy, which replaced the National Defense Program Guidelines, sets objectives for national defence and outlines how Japan will achieve them. The National Defense Program Guidelines, which were first published in 1976,

provided the doctrinal framework for the Medium Term Defense Program. The Defense Buildup Program, which replaced the Medium Term Defense Program, outlines defence spending and procurement over a five- to ten-year horizon.

15   See 'U.S. Ambassador: Japan–U.S. Alliance Has Entered Era of "Projection" into Indo-Pacific', *Japan News by the Yomiuri Shimbun*, 4 September 2022, https://japannews.yomiuri.co.jp/business/yies/20220904-55938/https://japannews.yomiuri.co.jp/business/yies/20220904-55938/.

16   Japan, Cabinet Secretariat, 'National Security Strategy of Japan', pp. 4, 20.

17   *Ibid.*, pp. 19–20.

18   IISS, *The Military Balance 2024* (Abingdon: Routledge for the IISS, 2024), pp. 14, 19.

19   Japan, Cabinet Secretariat, 'National Security Strategy of Japan', p. 5.

20   See, for example, the answer Singapore's defence minister, Ng Eng Heng, gave to the author's question at the 2023 IISS Shangri-La Dialogue on how Japan could help promote security in the Asia-Pacific: 'Dr Ng stated that … some Asian countries still want Japan to take greater accountability post-World War II, as Germany has done so. Dr Ng suggested that Japan continue reassuring its neighbours on Japan's militarisation and growth and engage in minilateralism.' From IISS, *The IISS Shangri-La Dialogue*, September 2023, p. 67, https://www.iiss.org/globalassets/media-library---content--migration/files/shangri-la-dialogue/2023/iiss-sld-2023-report.pdf?fr=xKAE9_zU1NQ.

21   The 1959–60 protests against the revision of the US–Japan Security Treaty, known in Japan as the Anpo Protests, involved some 30 million people throughout the country and played a significant role in the resignation of then-prime minister

Kishi Nobusuke once he had secured parliamentary approval for the revision. See Nick Kapur, *Japan at the Crossroads: Conflict and Compromise After Anpo* (Cambridge, MA: Harvard University Press, 2018).

22 Christopher W. Hughes, 'Japan's "Three National Security Documents" and Defense Capabilities: Reinforcing a Radical Military Trajectory', *Journal of Japanese Studies*, vol. 50, no. 1, Winter 2024, p. 180.

23 Japan, Ministry of Defense, 'Defense Buildup Program', 16 December 2022, p. 17, https://www.mod.go.jp/j/policy/agenda/guideline/plan/pdf/program_en.pdf.

24 Japan, Ministry of Defense, 'Medium Term Defense Program (FY2019–FY2023)', 18 December 2018, https://warp.da.ndl.go.jp/info:ndljp/pid/11591426/www.mod.go.jp/j/approach/agenda/guideline/2019/pdf/chuki_seibi31-35_e.pdf.

25 Lotje Boswinkel, 'Forever Bound? Japan's Road to Self-defence and the US Alliance', *Survival: Global Politics and Strategy*, vol. 66, no. 3, June–July 2024, pp. 108–9.

26 See, for example, Admiral Dong Jun, Minister of National Defense, China, 'China's Approach to Global Security', IISS Shangri-La Dialogue 2024, 2 June 2024, https://www.iiss.org/events/shangri-la-dialogue/shangri-la-dialogue-2024/plenary-sessions/fifth-plenary/.

27 A. Doak Barnett, *China and the Major Powers in East Asia* (Washington DC: The Brookings Institution, 1977), p. 35.

28 Edward Friedman, 'China's Changing Taiwan Policy', *American Journal of Chinese Studies*, vol. 14, no. 2, October 2007, p. 123.

29 Ezra F. Vogel, *China and Japan: Facing History* (Cambridge, MA and London: The Belknap Press of Harvard University Press, 2019), pp. 181, 353.

30 *Ibid.*, p. 130.

31 China, State Council, 'Proposal of the CPC Central Committee on the Formulation of the 14th Five-year Plan for National Economic and Social Development and the Long-term Goals for 2035', 3 November 2020, https://www.gov.cn/zhengce/2020-11/03/content_5556991.htm (translation from Chinese into English obtained using automated translation). Xi was not the first Chinese leader to call for 'the great rejuvenation of the Chinese nation' – Hu Jintao and Jiang Zemin also used this formulation and Deng Xiaoping called for the 'invigoration of China'. See Council on Foreign Relations, 'Excerpt: The Third Revolution', 2018, https://www.cfr.org/excerpt-third-revolution.

32 Bonnie S. Glaser, 'The Deteriorating US–China Relationship and the Indo-Pacific', in *Asia-Pacific Regional Security Assessment 2020: Key Developments and Trends* (Abingdon: Routledge for the IISS, 2021), p. 11.

33 Helen Davidson, 'China Warns of Reprisals Against Taiwan After President's Inauguration Speech', *Guardian*, 22 May 2024, https://www.theguardian.com/world/article/2024/may/22/china-warns-of-reprisals-against-taiwan-after-presidents-inauguration-speech.

34 Katya Golubkova, 'How Great Is Japan's Reliance on the Middle East Energy [sic]', Reuters, 27 October 2023, https://www.reuters.com/business/energy/how-great-is-japans-reliance-middle-east-energy-2023-10-27/#:~:text=CONCENTRATED%20CRUDE%20SOURCE,unique%20among%20major%20oil%20importers; and Kanehara Nobukatsu and Takamizawa Nobushige, *Kokka no Sōryoku* [The total power of the nation] (Tokyo: Shinchosha, 2024), p. 4.

35 Iwata Kiyofumi et al., *Kimi Tachi, Chūgoku ni Kateru no ka? Jieitai Saikō*

Kanbu ga Kataru Nichi Bei Dōmei vs Chūgoku [Guys, can we win against China? SDF top brass on the Japan–US alliance vs China] (Tokyo: Sankei Shimbun Shuppan, 2023), pp. 103–4.

36 Japan, Ministry of Foreign Affairs, 'Trends in China Coast Guard and Other Vessels in the Waters Surrounding the Senkaku Islands, and Japan's Response', https://www.mofa.go.jp/files/100647455.pdf.

37 'Tokyo to Buy Disputed Islands, Says Governor Ishihara', BBC News, 17 April 2012, https://www.bbc.co.uk/news/world-asia-17747934.

38 Robert Ward, 'Japan's Security and China', in *Asia-Pacific Regional Security Assessment 2021: Key Developments and Trends* (Abingdon: Routledge for the IISS, 2021), pp. 31–2.

39 Japan, Cabinet Secretariat, 'National Security Strategy of Japan', p. 1.

40 Japan, Ministry of Foreign Affairs, 'Keynote Address, Friday 10 June 2022, Fumio Kishida, Prime Minister of Japan', https://www.mofa.go.jp/files/100356160.pdf.

41 Kentaro Iwamoto, 'Japan PM Kishida Arrives in Kyiv for Talks with Zelenskyy', *Nikkei Asia*, 21 March 2023, https://asia.nikkei.com/Politics/Ukraine-war/Japan-PM-Kishida-arrives-in-Kyiv-for-talks-with-Zelenskyy.

42 IISS, *Strategic Survey 2022: The Annual Assessment of Geopolitics* (Abingdon: Routledge for the IISS, 2022), p. 41.

43 SWIFT stands for Society for Worldwide Interbank Financial Telecommunication.

44 Ruxandra Iordache and Holly Ellyatt, '"Russia has to pay": G7 Taps Moscow's Frozen Assets in Support of Ukraine', CNBC, 14 June 2024, https://www.cnbc.com/2024/06/14/russia-has-to-pay-g7-taps-moscows-frozen-assets-in-support-of-ukraine.html.

45 IISS, *Strategic Survey 2022*, p. 67.

46 For a full list of participants in the G7 Hiroshima Summit, see Japan, Ministry of Foreign Affairs, 'Participants', https://www.mofa.go.jp/policy/economy/summit/hiroshima23/en/summit/members/.

47 Robert Gilpin, *War and Change in World Politics* (Cambridge: Cambridge University Press, 1981), p. 198.

48 Richard Overy, *Why War?* (London: Pelican Books, 2024), p. 261.

49 Gilpin, *War and Change in World Politics*, p. 198.

50 Bernard Orr, Guy Faulconbridge and Andrew Osborn, 'Putin and Xi Pledge a New Era and Condemn the United States', Reuters, 17 May 2024, https://www.reuters.com/world/putin-visit-chinas-xi-deepen-strategic-partnership-2024-05-15/; and Simone McCarthy, 'No Path to Peace: Five Key Takeaways from Xi and Putin's Talks in Moscow', CNN, 22 March 2023, https://edition.cnn.com/2023/03/22/europe/china-xi-russia-putin-talks-five-takeaways-intl-hnk-mic/index.html.

51 For examples of Russian–Chinese joint patrols and exercises, see Robert Ward and Yuka Koshino, 'Japan Steps Up: Security and Defence Policy Under Kishida', in *Asia-Pacific Regional Security Assessment 2023: Key Developments and Trends* (Abingdon: Routledge for the IISS, 2023), p. 119.

52 Jean Mackenzie, 'North Korean Weapons Are Killing Ukrainians. The Implications Are Far Bigger', BBC News, 4 May 2024, https://www.bbc.co.uk/news/world-asia-68933778.

53 Hattori Ryuji, *Nakasone Yasuhiro, 'Daitōryōteki Shushō' no Kiseki* [Nakasone Yasuhiro, trajectory of a 'presidential prime minister'] (Tokyo: Chuo Koron Shinsha, 2015), pp. 214–15. Prime minister Ohira Masayoshi had also described Japan as an 'unsinkable aircraft carrier' for the US during a visit to meet with then-president Jimmy Carter in May 1979.

This came in response to US calls for Japan to increase military spending, so had a less forward-leaning military context. See Hattori Ryuji, *Zōho Ban, Ōhira Masayoshi, Rinen to Gaikō* [Expanded edition: Ohira Masayoshi – philosophy and diplomacy] (Tokyo: Bungei Shunjū, 2019), pp. 175–6.

54 Joachim Glaubitz, *Between Tokyo and Moscow: The History of an Uneasy Relationship, 1972 to the 1990s* (London: C. Hurst & Co., 1995), pp. 37–8.

55 Suzuki Yoshikatsu, *Hoppō Ryōdo Kōshō Shi* [History of the Northern Territories negotiations] (Tokyo: Chikuma Shinsho, 2021), pp. 250–1. In the 1990s, then-president Boris Yeltsin's administration appeared to indicate some Russian flexibility on the issue, but this was not sustained when Vladimir Putin took over as Russian president in 2000.

56 Hasegawa Tsuyoshi, *Hoppō Ryōdo Mondai to Nichi Ro Kankei* [The Northern Territories issue and Japan–Russia relations] (Tokyo: Chikuma Shobo, 2000), p. 38.

57 North Korea's missile 'tests' are widely seen as drills intended to operationalise the country's missile-launch capabilities. See, for example, 'Japan's Approaches to Nuclear Non-proliferation and Deterrence with Akiyama Nobumasa and William Alberque', Japan Memo podcast, IISS, 18 April 2023, https://www.iiss.org/podcasts/japan-memo/2023/04/japans-approaches-to-nuclear-non-proliferation-and-deterrence-with-akiyama-nobumasa-and-william-alberque/. For a map of recent North Korean and Chinese missile tests in Japan's direction, see Ward and Koshino, 'Japan Steps Up: Security and Defence Policy Under Kishida', p. 120. See also Jesse Johnson, 'Japan Says Five Chinese Ballistic Missiles Landed Inside EEZ Near Okinawa', *Japan Times*, 4 August 2022, https://www.japantimes.co.jp/news/2022/08/04/national/japan-china-missiles-eez/#:~:text=Japan%20says%20five%20Chinese%20ballistic%20missiles%20landed%20inside%20EEZ%20near%20Okinawa,-A%20screenshot%20of&text=Five%20ballistic%20missiles%20launched%20by,Defense%20Minister%20Nobuo%20Kishi%20said.

58 For a detailed discussion of China's and Russia's approaches to alliances, see IISS, 'Changing Alliance Structures', December 2021, pp. 11–19, https://www.iiss.org/globalassets/media-library---content--migration/files/research-papers/2021/alliances-report.pdf.

59 At a special session of the 2023 IISS Shangri-La Dialogue, Cui Tiankai, formerly China's vice minister of foreign affairs, referred to this loss of Chinese territory to Russia, indicating that China still believed that 'all these treaties were imposed on China, they were unfair treaties'. See IISS, '20th Asia Security Summit: The Shangri-La Dialogue: Special Sessions – Session 5 – Q&A', 3 June 2023, p. 10, https://www.iiss.org/events/shangri-la-dialogue/shangri-la-dialogue-2023/special-sessions/. The border between the two countries was formally fixed, finally, in 2004. See 'Putin and Hu Resolve Border Disputes', *New York Times*, 15 October 2004, https://www.nytimes.com/2004/10/15/world/asia/putin-and-hu-resolve-border-disputes.html.

60 Sergey Radchenko, *To Rule the World; The Kremlin's Cold War Bid for Global Power* (Cambridge: Cambridge University Press, 2024), p. 187.

61 Isaac B. Kardon, *China's Law of the Sea: The New Rules of Maritime Order* (New Haven, CT: Yale University Press, 2023), p. 2. Brunei, Malaysia and Vietnam also dispute maritime territory with China.

62 *Ibid.*, p. 5.

63 Admiral Dong Jun, 'China's Approach to Global Security'.

64 Admiral Dong Jun's criticism of freedom-of-navigation activities when speaking at the 2024 Shangri-La Dialogue was emblematic of this. See *Ibid*.

65 For an excellent overview of the internationalism of Maoism, see Julia Lovell, *Maoism, A Global History* (London: The Bodley Head, 2019), for example, pp. 16–17.

66 Ambassador Mark A. Green, 'Debt Distress on the Road to "Belt and Road"', Wilson Center, 16 January 2024, https://www.wilsoncenter. org/blog-post/debt-distress-road-belt-and-road; and 'China's Belt and Road Initiative: A Geopolitical and Geo-economic Assessment', IISS, November 2022, pp. 21–2, 199–201, 246–7.

67 'Full Text: Keynote Speech by Chinese President Xi Jinping at APEC CEO Dialogues', XinhuaNet, 19 November 2020, http://www.xinhuanet.com/ english/2020-11/19/c_139527192.htm.

68 Steve Tsang and Olivia Cheung, *The Political Thought of Xi Jinping* (Oxford: Oxford University Press, 2024), p. 170.

69 *Ibid*., pp. 10, 168. *Tianxia* is an 'idealized Sino-centric view of inter-state relations' (p. 168).

70 Since 2010, Australia, Japan, Lithuania, the Philippines, South Korea and Taiwan have all been targets of Chinese economic coercion.

71 Koshino and Ward, *Japan's Effectiveness as a Geo-economic Actor: Navigating Great-power Competition*, p. 28.

72 Christopher Howe, *The Origins of Japanese Trade Supremacy, Development and Technology in Asia from 1540 to the Pacific War* (London: Hurst & Company, 1996), p. 337.

73 J.M. Roberts, *The Penguin History of the World* (London: Penguin, 1995), p. 817.

74 For a useful comparison of Japanese and Chinese modernisation efforts, see Vogel, *China and Japan: Facing History*, pp. 69–72.

75 Kitaoka Shinichi, *Kokuren no Seiji Rikigaku, Nihon wa Doko ni Iru no Ka* [The political dynamics of the United Nations, where is Japan?] (Tokyo: Chuo Koron Shinsha, 2013), pp. 4–5.

76 Liang Pan, *The United Nations in Japan's Foreign and Security Policymaking, 1945–1992: National Security, Party Politics, and International Status* (Cambridge, MA and London: Harvard University Asia Center of Harvard University Press, 2005), p. 6.

77 Vogel, *China and Japan: Facing History*, p. 342.

78 See, for example, '99.2% in Japan View China Unfavourably, Says Japan–China Public Opinion Survey', *Japan News by the Yomiuri Shimbun*, 11 October 2023, https://japannews. yomiuri.co.jp/politics/politics-government/20231011-142389/.

79 '84% of People Nationwide Say They Feel Japan's National Security Is Under Threat', *Japan News by the Yomiuri Shimbun*, 8 April 2024, https:// japannews.yomiuri.co.jp/politics/ defense-security/20240408-179132/.

80 White House, 'U.S.–Japan Joint Leaders' Statement: "U.S.–JAPAN GLOBAL PARTNERSHIP FOR A NEW ERA"', 16 April 2021, https://www.mofa.go.jp/ files/100177718.pdf.

81 'Kishi Bōeisō "Taiwan no Jōtai, Waga Kuni no Mondai", Ichimon Ittō' [Defence minister Kishi: 'Taiwan's situation is an issue for Japan', question and answer], *Nihon Keizai Shimbun*, 20 May 2021, https://www. nikkei.com/article/DGXZQOU A178FB0X10C21A5000000/. Kishi Nobuo is the brother of Abe Shinzo.

82 Ben Blanchard, 'Former PM Abe Says Japan, U.S. Could Not Stand By if China Attacked Taiwan', Reuters, 1 December 2021,

https://www.reuters.com/world/asia-pacific/former-pm-abe-says-japan-us-could-not-stand-by-if-china-attacked-taiwan-2021-12-01/.

83 See, for example, Satomi Minoru and Iwata Emi, '"Sengo de Ichiban Ii Kankei", Nihon no Giin Dan, Taiwan de Yūkō Enshutsu, Chūgoku wa Hanpatsu' [Japanese parliamentary group: 'The best relations since the war', a friendly performance in Taiwan draws China's anger], *Asahi Shimbun*, 21 May 2024, https://www.asahi.com/articles/ASS5N3RK7S5NUTFK00SM.html.

84 Sato Taketsugu, 'Hadome Naki "Bōeiryoku Kyōka" no Ayausa' [The danger of 'unrestrained strengthening of defence'], *Asahi Shimbun*, 30 June 2024, https://www.asahi.com/articles/DA3S15970813.html.

85 'Taiwan's Lai Seeks Unity in Talks with Veteran Japan Lawmaker Ishiba', Kyodo News, 13 August 2024, https://english.kyodonews.net/news/2024/08/37a4f375b555-taiwans-lai-seeks-unity-in-talks-with-veteran-japan-lawmaker-ishiba.html?phrase=tax%20relief&words=.

86 Robert Ward, 'Japan's Security Policy and China', *Asia-Pacific Regional Security Assessment 2021: Key Developments and Trends* (Abingdon: Routledge for the IISS, 2021), p. 32.

87 The Taiwan Relations Act stipulates, inter alia, that the US 'shall make available to Taiwan such defense articles and defense services in such quality as may be necessary to enable Taiwan to maintain a sufficient self-defense capacity', and that US policy 'shall maintain the capacity of the United States to resist any resort to force or other forms of coercion that would jeopardize the security, or social or economic system of the people of Taiwan'. See 'H.R.2479 – Taiwan Relations Act',

Congress.gov, https://www.congress.gov/bill/96th-congress/house-bill/2479.

88 For an outline of these conditions, see Japan, Ministry of Defense, 'Defense of Japan 2020', pp. 200–1, https://www.mod.go.jp/en/publ/w_paper/wp2020/pdf/R02020102.pdf.

89 *Ibid.*

90 Japan, Cabinet Secretariat, 'National Security Strategy of Japan', p. 3.

91 *Ibid.*, p. 3.

92 Colin S. Gray, 'Strategic Culture as Context: The First Generation of Theory Strikes Back', *Review of International Studies*, vol. 25, no. 1, January 1999, p. 50.

93 Dmitry (Dima) Adamsky, *The Russian Way of Deterrence: Strategic Culture, Coercion, and War* (Stanford, CA: Stanford University Press, 2023), p. 10.

94 For a detailed discussion of the differences between Japan and Germany in this respect, see Koshino and Ward, *Japan's Effectiveness as a Geo-economic Actor: Navigating Great-power Competition*, pp. 18–19.

95 Lloyd J. Austin III, Secretary of Defense, 'United States' Strategic Partnerships in the Indo-Pacific', IISS Shangri-La Dialogue 2024, Plenary Session 1, 1 June 2024, https://www.iiss.org/events/shangri-la-dialogue/shangri-la-dialogue-2024/plenary-sessions/first-plenary/.

96 Koji Sonoda and Daisuke Yajima, 'Yoshihide Yoshida: Top SDF Officer Vows to Deter Aggression in Indo-Pacific', *Asahi Shimbun*, 2 September 2024, https://www.asahi.com/ajw/articles/15410995.

97 United Kingdom, Ministry of Defence, Defence Secretary Grant Shapps, 'Defending Britain from a More Dangerous World', 15 January 2024, https://www.gov.uk/government/speeches/defending-britain-from-a-more-dangerous-world.

Chapter One

1   Nicholas J. Spykman, *America's Strategy in World Politics: The United States and the Balance of Power* (Abingdon: Routledge, 2017 [1942]), p. 41.

2   Kosaka Masataka, *Options for Japan's Foreign Policy*, Adelphi Paper 97 (London: IISS, 1973), republished in Robert Ward, Yuka Koshino and Matthieu Lebreton (eds), *Japan and the IISS: Connecting Western and Japanese Strategic Thought from the Cold War to the War on Ukraine* (Abingdon: Routledge for the IISS, 2023), p. 226.

3   Tara Subrajahiam, 'Japan Just Found 7,000 Islands It Didn't Know It Had', CNN, 3 March 2023, https://edition.cnn.com/2023/03/02/asia/japan-islands-double-report-intl-hnk/index.html.

4   Japan, Ministry of Foreign Affairs, 'Japanese Territory', https://www.mofa.go.jp/territory/page1we_000007.html#q2.

5   'How Remote Islands Underpin Japan's Maritime Power', *The Economist*, 19 October 2023, https://www.economist.com/asia/2023/10/19/how-remote-islands-underpin-japans-maritime-power. Maritime area includes territorial sea and exclusive economic zones. The top five countries in terms of maritime area are, in descending order, the US, Australia, Indonesia, New Zealand and Canada. Japan also boasts the world's largest area of sea at a depth of 6,000 metres or more. See Udagawa Katsushi, *Ki ni Naru Nihon Chiri* [An intriguing guide to the geography of Japan] (Tokyo: Kadokawa, 2023), p. 114.

6   Perry's ships were known in Japan as 'black ships' (*kurofune*) because of their black hulls.

7   The *Shogun* was nominally the emperor's military deputy, but in practice ruled Japan through the Shogun's *Bakufu* administration. The first *Shogun* was Minamato Yoritomo, who received the title from the emperor in 1192. The last, Tokugawa Yoshinobu, resigned from the position in 1868, surrendering Edo Castle without a fight.

8   Iriye Akira, *Nihon no Gaikō* [Japan's diplomacy] (Tokyo: Chuo Koron Shinsha, 2016), p. 18. In Japanese the quotation is: '*kaigai kakkoku to heiritsu wo hakaru*'.

9   Hideichi Horie, 'Revolution and Reform in Meiji Restoration', *Kyoto University Economic Review*, vol. 22, no. 1, April 1952, p. 23.

10 Michael Mandelbaum, *The Ideas That Conquered the World: Peace, Democracy and Free Markets in the Twenty-first Century* (New York: PublicAffairs, 2002), p. 80.

11 J.M. Roberts, *The Penguin History of the World* (London: Penguin, 1995), p. 812.

12 Five countries signed such treaties with Japan: the US, the UK, France, the Netherlands and Russia. See Iriye, *Nihon no Gaikō* [Japan's diplomacy], p. 18.

13 W.G. Beasley, *Japanese Imperialism, 1894–1945* (Oxford: Clarendon Press, 1987), pp. 25, 33–4. It should also be noted, however, that Japan imposed its own unequal treaty on Korea, the Treaty of Kanghwa, in 1876, and later did the same to China.

14 *Ibid.*, pp. 88–9.

15 For a useful account of Japan's ultimately disastrous road towards becoming a 'continental nation', see Iriye, *Nihon no Gaikō* [Japan's diplomacy], pp. 48–63.

16 *Ibid.*, p. 172.

17 S.C.M. Paine, *The Japanese Empire: Grand Strategy from the Meiji Restoration to the Pacific War* (Cambridge: Cambridge University Press, 2017), p. 118.

18 *Ibid.*, p. 103.

19 Iriye, *Nihon no Gaikō* [Japan's diplomacy], p. 144. *'Ajia no ichi taikoku taru Nihon wo, shōkoku, ichi shimaguni ni suru.'*

20 John Dower, *Embracing Defeat: Japan and the Aftermath of World War II* (London: Penguin Books, 1999), p. 77.

21 Sakaiya Shiro, *Sengo Nihon Seiji Shi, Senryōki Kara 'Neo' 55 Taisei Made* [Post-war Japan's political history: from the occupation to the 'neo'-1955 system] (Tokyo: Chuo Koron Shinsha, 2023), p. 13: '*Haisen kara dokuritsu made wa wazuka ni 7 nen kan de wa atta ga, kono aida no kuni no kaikaku wa osoraku rekishi ga shizen ni nagarete ita naraba, hyaku nen wo motte shite mo enakatta tokoro de arō*' [Just seven years separated wartime defeat and independence, but if the reforms undertaken in Japan had taken a natural historical course, even 100 years would probably not have been enough to bring them about].

22 *Ibid.*, p. 23.

23 Kenneth B. Pyle, *The Making of Modern Japan* (Lexington, MA and Toronto: D.C. Heath and Company, 1996), p. 219; and William Manchester, *American Caesar: Douglas MacArthur 1880–1964* (New York, Boston, MA and London: Little, Brown and Company, 1978), p. 500.

24 Manchester, *American Caesar: Douglas MacArthur 1880–1964*, p. 501.

25 Kosaka Masataka, *Options for Japan's Foreign Policy, Adelphi Papers*, no. 97, 1973, republished in Ward, Koshino and Lebreton (eds), *Japan and the IISS*, p. 205. In early 2024, all but one of the LDP's factions announced their dissolution in order to assuage public anger in the wake of a party-funding scandal.

26 Kenneth B. Pyle, *Japan Rising: The Resurgence of Japanese Power and Purpose* (New York: PublicAffairs, 2007), p. 15.

27 Sakaiya Shiro, *Sengo Nihon Seiji Shi, Senryōki Kara 'Neo' 55 Taisei Made* [Post-war Japan's political history: from the occupation to the 'neo'-1955 system], pp. 42–3.

28 Until early 2024, when a funding scandal triggered the dissolution of most of the LDP's factions, the factions had provided the party's organising structure and an important source of patronage. The LDP was thus essentially a federation of factions. It is currently unclear whether the factions will eventually reform, as was the case after previous dissolutions in the 1970s and 1990s.

29 Tobias Harris, *The Iconoclast: Shinzo Abe and the New Japan* (London: C. Hurst & Co., 2020), p. 188.

30 Yoshida's comments on Japan as a maritime nation are worth quoting in full: '*Nihon wa kaiyō kokka de ari, kaigai to no bōeki wo tsūjite, kyū sen man kokumin wo yashinawaneba naranai koto wa, akiraka de aru. Sō de aru ijō wa, Nihon no tsūshō jō no tsunagari wa, keizaiteki ni mo motto mo yūtaka na, soshite gijutsuteki ni mo ichi ban susunde ori, katsu rekishiteki ni mo kankei no fukai Bei Ei ryō koku ni onozu to omoki wo okazaru wo enai de wa nai ka.*' [It is clear that Japan is a maritime country and must feed its 90 million citizens through trade with other countries. As long as this is the case, Japan's trade ties naturally place emphasis on the US and the UK, which are the richest economically, the most advanced technologically and have deep historical ties.] Yoshida Shigeru, *Kaisō Jū Nen* [Ten years' reminiscence] (Tokyo: Mainichi Wanz, 2022), p. 22.

31 'Report on the Pacific Basin Cooperation Concept', 19 May 1980, 'The World and Japan' Database, Database of Japanese Politics and International Relations, National Graduate Institute for Policy Studies (GRIPS), Institute for Advanced Studies on Asia (IASA), The University of Tokyo, https://worldjpn. net/documents/texts/APEC/19800519. O1E.html.

32 Steven R. Weisman, 'Japanese Premier Vows "Even Greater Efforts" on Defense', *New York Times*, 9 May 1981, https://www.nytimes.com/1981/05/09/world/japanese-premier-vows-even-greater-efforts-on-defense.html.

33 For an account of the Reagan administration's push in the early 1980s for Japan to take on a greater role in defending sea lines of communication, see Tsuyoshi Hasegawa, 'The Soviet Factor in U.S.–Japanese Defense Cooperation, 1978–1985', *Journal of Cold War Studies*, vol. 15, no. 2, Spring 2013, pp. 87–93.

34 See, for example, Abe Shinzo, *Utsukushii Kuni E* [Towards a beautiful country] (Tokyo: Bunshun Shinsho, 2006), pp. 146–56.

35 Abe Shinzo, 'Asia's Democratic Security Diamond', Project Syndicate, 27 December 2012, https://www.project-syndicate.org/magazine/a-strategic-alliance-for-japan-and-india-by-shinzo-abe.

36 Japan, Ministry of Foreign Affairs, 'The 13th Shangri-La Dialogue Keynote Address by Shinzo Abe, Prime Minister of Japan', 30 May 2014, https://www.mofa.go.jp/fp/nsp/page4e_000086.html.

37 Michio Royama, *The Asian Balance of Power: A Japanese View*, Adelphi Papers, no. 42 (London: IISS, 1967), republished in Ward, Koshino and Lebreton (eds), *Japan and the IISS*, pp. 121–2.

38 A. Doak Barnett, *China and the Major Powers in East Asia* (Washington DC: The Brookings Institution, 1977), p. 89.

39 Sadako Ogata, 'The Japanese Attitude Towards China', *Asian Survey*, vol. 5, no. 8, August 1965, pp. 389–98, republished in *Survival: Global Politics and Strategy*, vol. 7, no. 9, 1965, and in Ward, Koshino and Lebreton (eds), *Japan and the IISS*, p. 86. See also Ezra F. Vogel, *China and Japan: Facing History* (Cambridge, MA and London:

40 The Belknap Press of Harvard University Press, 2019), p. vii.

40 Paine, *The Japanese Empire: Grand Strategy from the Meiji Restoration to the Pacific War*, p. 15.

41 For an on-the-ground account of what Byas called Japan's 'gangster decade', see Hugh Byas, *Government by Assassination* (New York: Alfred A. Knopf, 1942). The book is now available from the Eschenburg Press.

42 Cited by Funabashi Yoichi in 'Foreign Policy Requires a Keen Sense of Balance', *Japan Times*, 10 February 2017, https://www.japantimes.co.jp/opinion/2017/02/10/commentary/japan-commentary/foreign-policy-requires-keen-sense-balance/.

43 J.W. Dower, *Empire and Aftermath: Yoshida Shigeru and the Japanese Experience, 1878–1954* (Boston, MA: Council on East Asian Studies, Harvard University Press, 1988), pp. 37, 401.

44 Yoshida Shigeru, 'Japan and the Crisis in Asia', *Foreign Affairs*, 1 January 1951, https://www.foreignaffairs.com/articles/j Kosaka Masataka apan/1951-01-01/japan-and-crisis-asia.

45 Michael Schaller, *Altered States: The United States and Japan Since the Occupation* (New York and Oxford: Oxford University Press, 1997), p. 34.

46 For an account of the development of so-called LT and MT trade between Japan and China in the 1960s, see Hattori Kenji and Marukawa Tomoo (eds), *Nicchū Kankei Shi: 1972–2012, II Keizai* [History of Japan–China relations, 1972–2012, vol. II Economy] (Tokyo: Tokyo University Press, 2012), pp. 9–14.

47 Odd Arne Westad and Chen Jian, *The Great Transformation: China's Road from Revolution to Reform* (New Haven, CT and London: Yale University Press, 2024), pp. 42–3.

48 Tanaka Akihiko, *Nicchū Kankei 1945–1990* [Japan–China relations,

1945–1990] (Tokyo: University of Tokyo Press, 1991), p. 13.

49   Prime minister Sato Eisaku struggled to recalibrate Japanese policy towards China after the first 1971 'Nixon shock', which came with Nixon's announcement that the US intended to normalise US–China relations. These difficulties reflected diplomatic contortions around Tokyo's policy towards China's accession to the United Nations and the expulsion of Taiwan. However, the Nixon shock had also increased the importance of relations with China in Japanese foreign policy, and the 1972 LDP election to replace Sato was the first leadership contest where great importance was given to the issue. Miki Takeo, on the party's progressive wing – himself a candidate for prime minister in 1972, and for prime minister after Tanaka Kakuei's fall from power – was among those most strongly in favour of closer relations between Japan and China. As well as cultivating political links with the Japan Communist Party and the Socialist Party, China had also worked to forge links with senior members of Japan's conservative parties. See Robert Hoppens, *The China Problem in Postwar Japan: Japanese National Identity and Sino-Japanese Relations* (London: Bloomsbury, 2015), pp. 76–9, for a discussion of Japan's diplomatic difficulties with China in the wake of the first Nixon shock. See Barnett, *China and the Major Powers in East Asia*, pp. 95–7, 111, for a discussion of China's efforts to develop political ties with Japan from the 1950s onwards, including in the 1970s.

50   Hoppens, *The China Problem in Postwar Japan: Japanese National Identity and Sino-Japanese Relations*, p. 80. See also Hayano Toru, *Tanaka Kakuei, Sengo Nihon no Kanashiki Jigazō* [Tanaka Kakuei, a sad self-portrait of post-war

Japan] (Tokyo: Chuo Koron Shinsha, 2021), p. 232.

51   Hoppens, *The China Problem in Postwar Japan: Japanese National Identity and Sino-Japanese Relations*, p. 110.

52   Ever attentive to the domestic audience, Tanaka, like Nixon, ensured that his visit to Beijing was broadcast by television stations back home. Using equipment taken to Beijing for the occasion, this was Japanese television's first satellite broadcast from China.

53   Richard M. Nixon, 'Asia After Viet Nam', *Foreign Affairs*, 1 October 1967, https://www.foreignaffairs.com/articles/united-states/1967-10-01/asia-after-viet-nam.

54   Richard Nixon, *RN: The Memoirs of Richard Nixon* (New York: Simon & Schuster, 1992), p. 542. China conducted its first nuclear test in 1964.

55   Westad and Chen, *The Great Transformation: China's Road from Revolution to Reform*, pp. 82–3.

56   Hoppens, *The China Problem in Postwar Japan: Japanese National Identity and Sino-Japanese Relations*, p. 132.

57   The Chinese had long accused the Soviet Union of 'hegemonism', or expansion of political and economic influence and control, in the region, and indeed make the same charge against the US today. The US and China had agreed on the 'anti-hegemony' formulation in the Shanghai Communiqué, issued by Nixon and Chinese premier Zhou Enlai when the former visited China in 1972. The communiqué called on the signatories to renounce 'hegemony' and to reject hegemony by other countries. The Japanese feared that the insertion of that clause into the treaty would both antagonise the Soviet Union and expose Japan to future criticism by China on account of its own activities in the region. See Zbigniew Brzezinski, *Power and Principle: Memoirs of the National*

Security Adviser, 1977–81 (New York: Farrar, Straus & Giroux, 1983), p. 218.

58 Henry Kissinger, *Leadership: Six Studies in World Strategy* (London: Allen Lane, 2022), p. 141.

59 For examples of how Deng Xiaoping viewed the Soviet Union, see Ezra F. Vogel, *Deng Xiaoping and the Transformation of China* (Cambridge, MA: The Belknap Press of Harvard University Press, 2011), pp. 153–5, 269–70.

60 Odd Arne Westad, *The Cold War: A World History* (London: Allen Lane, 2017), p. 489. See also pp. 484–92 in the volume for an account of how US– Soviet relations deteriorated under the Carter administration. A. Doak Barnett refers to the LDP's desire to maintain 'equidistance' between China and the Soviet Union at this time in *China and the Major Powers in East Asia*, p. 127.

61 Hoppen, *The China Problem in Postwar Japan: Japanese National Identity and Sino-Japanese Relations*, p. 194.

62 *Ibid.*

63 For a discussion of Gorbachev's 'new thinking', see Peter Zwick, 'New Thinking and New Foreign Policy Under Gorbachev', *PS: Political Science and Politics*, vol. 22, no. 2, June 1989.

64 For a detailed account of how Japan violated COCOM rules, see Yuka Koshino and Robert Ward, *Japan's Effectiveness as a Geo-economic Actor: Navigating Great-power Competition*, Adelphi 481–483 (Abingdon: Routledge for the IISS, 2022), p. 41.

65 'Peace and Security for the Asia-Pacific Ocean Region. Excerpt from Speech by Mikhail Gorbachev in Vladivostok, 28 July 1986', *Contemporary Southeast Asia*, Yusof Ishak Institute, vol. 8, no. 3, December 1986, pp. 250–8. Key elements of Gorbachev's outreach to China were the announcements in the Vladivostok speech that the Soviet Union would reduce its military presence in Afghanistan and Mongolia, and the suggestion of settling the Sino-Soviet dispute concerning the Amur River border. The CIA noted that these were 'the most far-reaching proposals toward bettering relations with China a Soviet leader has made in public since the Sino-Soviet split': CIA, Directorate of Intelligence, 'USSR – Gorbachev's Speech on Asian Security', 28 July 1986, https://www.cia.gov/readingroom/docs/CIA-RDP91B00874R000100220011-6.pdf.

66 Hasegawa Tsuyoshi, *Hoppō Ryōdo Mondai to Nichi Ro Kankei* [The Northern Territories issue and Japan–Russia relations] (Tokyo: Chikuma Shobo, 2000), pp. 96–7.

67 US Office of the Historian, Helsinki Final Act, 1975, https://history.state.gov/milestones/1969-1976/helsinki#:~:text=Every%20European%20country%20except%20Albania,the%20United%20States%20and%20Canada.

68 Hasegawa, *Hoppō Ryōdo Mondai to Nichi Ro Kankei* [The Northern Territories issue and Japan–Russia relations], p. 120.

69 Abe described Sino-Japanese relations as 'inseverable': '*Nihon to Chūgoku wa kitte mo kirenai "gokei no kankei" ni aru no wa ron wo matanai*' [It is beyond argument that Japan–China relations are 'inseverable and reciprocal']. See Abe, *Utsukushii Kuni E* [Towards a beautiful country], p. 151. Also of interest is the recording of a conversation between H.R. McMaster and Abe Shinzo: 'Japan: The Legacy of Japan's Longest Serving Prime Minister', Battlegrounds with H.R. McMaster, Hoover Institution, 21 July 2021, https://www.hoover.org/research/japan-legacy-japans-longest-serving-prime-minister. (At 9:25 minutes, Abe said: 'When we look back at history we see many instances and cases where one side had a misunderstanding and

underestimated the will and capability of the other side, and that eventually led to confrontation or disputes. So, in that context, I do believe that it remains very important for us to make China realise Japan's determination and also have a correct understanding about Japan's capability, and that will remain the key.')

70 Suzuki Yoshikatsu, *Hoppō Ryōdo Kōshō Shi* [History of the Northern Territories negotiations] (Tokyo: Chikuma Shinsho, 2021), p. 68.

71 Hashimoto Koro, Oyama Hiroshi and Kitamura Shigeru (eds), Abe Shinzo, *Abe Shinzō Kaiko Roku* [Abe Shinzo's memoirs] (Tokyo: Chuo Koron Shinsha, 2023), pp. 215–19.

72 *Ibid*., pp. 326–32. See 'Joint Declaration by the Union of Soviet Socialist Republics and Japan', 19 October 1956, 'The World and Japan' Database, National Graduate Institute for Policy Studies, Institute for Advanced Studies on Asia, The University of Tokyo, https://worldjpn.net/documents/texts/docs/19561019.D1E.html. The Soviet position on the Habomai Islands and Shikotan changed after the revision of the US–Japan security treaty in 1960. See Joachim Glaubitz, *Between Tokyo and Moscow: The History of an Uneasy Relationship, 1972 to the 1990s* (London: C. Hurst & Co., 1995), p. 43.

73 Glaubitz, *Between Tokyo and Moscow: The History of an Uneasy Relationship, 1972 to the 1990s*, p. 43.

74 'Abe May Settle for Return of Just 2 out of 4 Northern Territories from Russia', *Mainichi*, 23 November 2018, https://mainichi.jp/english/articles/20181123/p2a/00m/0na/006000c.

75 'Hoppō Ryōdo "Fuhō Senkyo" Gaikō Seisho de 03 Nen Irai no Fukkatsu' ['Illegal occupation' used in Diplomatic Blue Book for first time since 2003], *Nihon Keizai Shimbun*, 31 March 2022, https://www.nikkei.com/article/DGXZQOUA30DK00Q2A330C2000000/.

76 See, for example, Abe's comments in this article: '"Chū Ro ga Te wo Kumu Jitai Dake wa Sakeneba" Abe Shushō ga Mezasu Nichi Ro Shin Jidai to wa' ['It is important to avoid China and Russia working together', Prime Minister Abe's aim for the new era of Japan–Russia Relations], *Sankei Shimbun*, 23 January 2019, https://www.sankei.com/article/20190123-SW72VPRMOJNULCOXYF463W2QPI/. See also Abe's comments in this interview in a publication produced by Japan's Ministry of Foreign Affairs: '"Jiyū de Hirakareta Indo-Taiheyō" ni Miru Senryakuteki Shikō' [Strategic thinking in the 'free and open Indo-Pacific'], *Gaikō* [Diplomacy], vol. 65, January–February 2021, p. 97.

77 'Shushō, Chū Ro Kantai "Fuon na Ugoki", Nihon Rettō wo Hobo Isshū' [Prime minister calls out 'unsettling movements' of Sino-Russian fleet, which almost circles Japanese archipelago], *Nihon Keizai Shimbun*, 25 October 2021, https://www.nikkei.com/article/DGXZQOUA2570L0V21C21A0000000/.

78 'Taiwan Says It Spots Two Russian Warships off Its East Coast', Reuters, 27 June 2023, https://www.reuters.com/world/taiwan-says-it-spots-two-russian-warships-off-its-east-coast-2023-06-27/.

79 Japan, Ministry of Defense, 'Defense of Japan 2024', Annual White Paper, p. 18, https://www.mod.go.jp/en/publ/w_paper/index.html.

80 Nigel Gould-Davies, 'Russia, the West and Sanctions', *Survival: Global Politics and Strategy*, vol. 62, no. 1, February–March 2020, p. 10.

81 Japan, Cabinet Secretariat, 'National Security Strategy of Japan', December 2022, p. 1.

Chapter Two

1   Colin S. Gray, *The Geopolitics of Super Power* (Lexington, KY: The University Press of Kentucky, 1988), p. 21.

2   James Kynge, 'China Is Tightening Its Embrace with Russia as It Builds Bulwarks Against the West', *Financial Times*, 24 March 2023, https://www.ft.com/content/bbaa4006-318e-4dbe-b7d4-3c21aa5e8887.

3   In *White House Years*, Henry Kissinger writes of the United States' military bases in Okinawa that 'we counted on its airfields for the defense of Korea and Taiwan; we used it as a staging area for Vietnam as an emergency facility for B-52s'. Henry Kissinger, *White House Years* (New York: Simon and Schuster, 2011), pp. 458–9.

4   'US Believed It Would 'Undoubtedly Win' War with North Korea in 1994 – but with Huge Casualties', *Guardian*, 8 December 2017, https://www.theguardian.com/world/2017/dec/08/pentagon-believed-it-would-undoubtedly-win-war-with-north-korea-in-1994.

5   See Japan, Ministry of Defense, 'The Guidelines for Japan–US Defense Cooperation', https://www.mod.go.jp/en/j-us-alliance/guidelines/index.html, for links to the 1978, 1997 and 2015 guidelines.

6   Yew Lun Tian and Ben Blanchard, 'China Will Never Renounce Right to Use Force Over Taiwan, Xi Says', Reuters, 16 October 2022, https://www.reuters.com/world/china/xi-china-will-never-renounce-right-use-force-over-taiwan-2022-10-16/. See also comments by Professor Michishita Narushige, Executive Vice President and Professor at the National Graduate Institute for Policy Studies (GRIPS), 'Changes in Japan's Defence Industry', IISS Japan Chair Programme webinar, 3 July 2024, https://www.iiss.org/events/2024/062/changes-in-japans-defence-industry/.

7   Chijiwa Yasuaki, *Nichibei Dōmei to Chiseigaku – '5tsu no Shikaku' wo Toinaosu* [The geopolitics of the Japan–US alliance – reassessing five blind spots] (Tokyo: Shinchosha, 2024), p. 9. In a conversation that this author had during this writing, a former senior member of the Japan Self-Defense Forces (SDF) contrasted policymakers' current concerns about civilians' safety with the failure of the Japanese authorities to protect its civilians during the Second World War. By the end of the Second World War, 66 Japanese cities had been reduced to rubble, with only Kyoto, Nara and Kanazawa surviving intact. See S.C.M. Paine, *The Japanese Empire: Grand Strategy from the Meiji Restoration to the Pacific War* (Cambridge: Cambridge University Press, 2017), p. 165. The Toyama Official City Travel Guide describes Toyama in central Japan as the most heavily bombed of all the country's cities in the war.

8   Robert Hoppens, *The China Problem in Postwar Japan: Japanese National Identity and Sino-Japanese Relations* (London: Bloomsbury, 2015), p. 195.

9   Sheila Smith, *Japan Rearmed: The Politics of Military Power* (Cambridge, MA: Harvard University Press, 2019), pp. 205–6. For a discussion of Japanese public opinion at the time, see Joachim Glaubitz, *Between Tokyo and Moscow: The History of an Uneasy Relationship, 1972 to the 1990s* (London: C. Hurst & Co., 1995), pp. 198–201.

10 Hyonhee Shin, Josh Smith and Kantaro Komiya, 'North Korea Conducts Longest-range Missile Test Yet Over Japan', Reuters, 4 October 2022, https://www.reuters.com/world/asia-pacific/nkorea-fires-missile-towards-east-skorea-military-2022-10-03/.

11 See Japan, Ministry of Defense, 'Defense of Japan 2023', https://www.mod.go.jp/en/publ/w_paper/wp2023/DOJ2023_EN_Full.pdf, p. 7, for a map of where the Chinese missiles landed. This incident also served to highlight yet another territorial fault line running between China on the one hand and Japan and other countries in the region on the other – that is, China's expansive calculations of its own maritime claims. China uses the principle of 'natural prolongation' while Japan, for example, calculates its EEZ using distanced- and continental-shelf-based calculations. In this case, China's claimed maritime entitlement extends into Japan's EEZ as far as the Okinawa Trough, a depression running from north to south in the East China Sea and lying closer to Japan than to China. China's claims significantly reduce the size of Japan's EEZ. See Isaac B. Kardon, *China's Law of the Sea: The New Rules of Maritime Order* (New Haven, CT: Yale University Press, 2023), pp. 104–6, for a useful discussion of the differences between how China and Japan measure their maritime entitlements.

12 See, for example, 'Sakishima Shotō no Hinan Keikaku, Seifu ga Sennin Han Setchi, Kaku Jichitai to Chōsei' [Planning for evacuation of the Sakishima Islands, the government establishes a dedicated team of experts and coordinates with each local government], *Nihon Keizai Shimbun*, 30 January 2024, https://www.nikkei.com/article/DGXZQOUA2260K0S4A120C2000000/.

13 'Why Japan Needs More Forceful Defence', *The Economist*, 7 December 2021, https://www.economist.com/special-report/2021/12/07/why-japan-needs-more-forceful-defence.

14 For a discussion on how and why Japanese submarines might be deployed in the area in the event of a Taiwan contingency, see Veerle Nouwens and Ken Moriyasu, 'Episode 20: Japan's Security in 2021: A New Defence White Paper', Bridging the Oceans podcast, RUSI, 21 July 2021, https://rusi.org/podcasts/bridging-the-oceans/episode-20-japans-security-2021-new-defence-white-paper (around 15:30 minutes into the podcast). The 2024 edition of the IISS *Military Balance* notes that Japan's Maritime Self-Defense Force (MSDF) possessed a fleet of 24 SSK submarines, of which there were ten *Oyashio*-class submarines, 12 *Soryu*-class submarines and two *Taigei*-class submarines. See *The Military Balance 2024* (Abingdon: Routledge for the IISS, 2024), p. 278.

15 'Japan's Amphibious Rapid Deployment Brigade', Grey Dynamics, 19 November 2021, https://greydynamics.com/japans-amphibious-rapid-deployment-brigade/.

16 Christopher W. Hughes, 'Japan's "Three National Security Documents" and Defense Capabilities: Reinforcing a Radical Military Trajectory', *Journal of Japanese Studies*, vol. 50, no. 1, Winter 2024, p. 77.

17 'Rikujō Jieitai, Nansei Shotō e Zen Butai Tenkai Kanō ni, Taiwan Yūji Sonae' [Japan Ground Self-Defense Force to be able to deploy all troops to the Nansei Islands in preparation for a Taiwan contingency], *Nihon Keizai Shimbun*, 3 January 2023, https://www.nikkei.com/article/DGXZQOUA283Z60Y2A221C2000000/.

18 Nagatomi Shinnojō, 'Jieitai, Mamori no Jūshin wo Nishi ni, 10 Nen de Okinawa no Shisetsu wa 4 Wari zō' [Self-Defense Forces shift centre of defence to the West, facilities in Okinawa increase by 40% in 10 years], *Nihon Keizai Shimbun*, 2 July 2024, https://www.nikkei.com/article/DGXZQOUA2417T0U4A620C2000000/.

19 Takeuchi Yusuke, 'Ishigaki Jima, Bōei Saizensen no Ima Nansei Shotō no "Kūhaku" Umaru' [Ishigaki Island, the current front line of defence, filling the 'void' in the Nansei Islands], *Nihon Keizai Shimbun*, 4 April 2023, https://www.nikkei.com/article/DGXZQOUA307Y30Q3A330C2000000/.

20 *Ibid.*

21 Michishita Narushige, 'Japan's Realism Diplomacy', Center for Strategic and International Studies, 8 June 2023, https://www.csis.org/analysis/japans-new-national-security-strategy#:~:text=Japan%20is%20acquiring%20strike%20capabilities,China%20even%20if%20it%20can.

22 Tajima Yoshihiko, 'Teki Kichi Kōgeki wa Gōken? Iken? Hitsuyō Saishōgen Hoka ni Shudan wa Nai to wa' [Is attacking enemy bases constitutional? Unconstitutional? What do 'minimum necessary' and 'no other option' mean?], *Asahi Shimbun*, 27 March 2023, https://www.asahi.com/articles/ASR3W5CQRR2WUTFK004.html.

23 Japan, Ministry of Defense, 'National Defense Program Guidelines for FY 2019 and Beyond', 18 December 2018, pp. 21–2, https://warp.da.ndl.go.jp/info:ndljp/pid/11591426/www.mod.go.jp/j/approach/agenda/guideline/2019/pdf/20181218_e.pdf.

24 Japan, Cabinet Secretariat, 'National Security Strategy of Japan', December 2022, pp. 19–20, https://www.cas.go.jp/jp/siryou/221216anzenhoshou/nss-e.pdf.

25 *Ibid.*, p. 19.

26 Jeffrey W. Hornung and Christopher B. Johnstone, 'Japan's Strategic Shift Is Significant, but Implementation Hurdles Await', War on the Rocks, 27 January 2023, https://warontherocks.com/2023/01/japans-strategic-shift-is-significant-but-implementation-hurdles-await/.

27 Lotje Boswinkel, 'Forever Bound? Japan's Road to Self-defence and the US Alliance', *Survival: Global Politics and Strategy*, vol. 66, no. 3, June–July 2024, pp. 105–6.

28 Robert Ward and Yuka Koshino, 'Japan Steps Up: Security and Defence Policy Under Kishida', in *Asia-Pacific Regional Security Assessment 2023: Key Developments and Trends* (Abingdon: Routledge for the IISS, 2023), p. 124.

29 *Ibid.*, p. 125.

30 C. Todd Lopez, 'U.S. Intends to Reconstitute U.S. Forces Japan as a Joint Forces Headquarters', US Department of Defense, 28 July 2024, https://www.defense.gov/News/News-Stories/Article/Article/3852213/us-intends-to-reconstitute-us-forces-japan-as-joint-forces-headquarters/.

31 Cathal J. Nolan, *The Allure of Battle: A History of How Wars Have Been Won and Lost* (Oxford: Oxford University Press, 2019), pp. 492–3.

32 Paine, *The Japanese Empire: Grand Strategy from the Meiji Restoration to the Pacific War*, p. 159.

33 Boswinkel, 'Forever Bound? Japan's Road to Self-defence and the US Alliance', p. 116.

34 Nolan, *The Allure of Battle: A History of How Wars Have Been Won and Lost*, p. 2.

35 See, for example, Eisuke Mori, 'Taiwan Yūji de Chūgoku wa Arayuru Odoshi wo Nihon ni Kakeru' [In the event of a Taiwan contingency, China will make all sorts of threats against Japan], *Nikkei Business*, 27 August 2021, https://business.nikkei.com/atcl/gen/19/00179/081600068/; and 'Taiwan Bōei, Bei Gun Shien ni "2–3 Shūkan", Moto Taiwan Gun Toppu "Jūrai Gata no Hensei, Tenkan wo"' [It could take US forces two to three weeks to come to Taiwan's defence: a former senior figure from Taiwan's military calls for an 'organisational shift'],

Nihon Keizai Shimbun, 4 November 2023, https://www.nikkei.com/article/DGKKZO75858720T01C23A1FF8000/.

36 Japan, Cabinet Secretariat, 'National Security Strategy of Japan', p. 27.

37 'Bōei Ryoku Kyōka e Kūkō, Minato wo Seibi, Nerai wa?' [What is the aim of developing airports and ports to strengthen defence capabilities?], *Nihon Keizai Shimbun*, 29 September 2023, https://www.nikkei.com/article/DGXZQODL28AOU0Y3A920C2000000/.

38 'Jieitai no Kayaku Ryōsan e Kuni ga Kōjō Kensetsu, Danyaku Fusoku ni Sonae' [Government to build factory to mass produce explosives for Self-Defense Forces in preparation for ammunition shortage], *Nihon Keizai Shimbun*, 17 September 2022, https://www.nikkei.com/article/DGXZQOUA142CA0U2A910C2000000/.

39 'Jieitai no Danyaku Ko, Nansei Shotō ni Bunsan e, Taiwan Yūji Nentō' [Self-Defense Forces ammunition depots to be dispersed among the Nansei Islands in case of a Taiwan contingency], *Nihon Keizai Shimbun*, 6 January 2023, https://www.nikkei.com/article/DGXZQOUA2844W0Y2A221C2000000/.

40 Yusuke Takeuchi, 'Japan Passes Defense Subsidy Bill to Stop Industry Bleeding', *Nikkei Asia*, 8 June 2023, https://asia.nikkei.com/Business/Aerospace-Defense-Industries/Japan-passes-defense-subsidy-bill-to-stop-industry-bleeding.

41 Boswinkel, 'Forever Bound? Japan's Road to Self-defence and the US Alliance', p. 119.

42 Yusuke Takeuchi, 'Japan Passes Defense Subsidy Bill to Stop Industry Bleeding'. See also Ishimaru Jumpei, 'New Opportunities and Old Constraints for Japan's Defence Industry', IISS Online Analysis, 19 August 2024,

https://www.iiss.org/online-analysis/online-analysis/2024/08/new-opportunities-and-old-constraints-for-japans-defence-industry/.

43 See comments by Sumomo Sayako, Director, International Cooperation Division, Department of Equipment Policy at the Acquisition, Technology and Logistics Agency, 'Changes in Japan's Defence Industry', IISS Japan Chair Programme webinar, 3 July 2024, https://www.iiss.org/events/2024/062/changes-in-japans-defence-industry/.

44 Tim Kelly, 'US Needs Japan's Help to Boost Military Production, Ambassador Says', Reuters, 10 June 2024, https://www.reuters.com/world/us-needs-japans-help-boost-military-production-ambassador-says-2024-06-10/.

45 See, for example, Japan, Cabinet Secretariat, 'National Security Strategy', 17 December 2013, p. 22, https://www.cas.go.jp/jp/siryou/131217anzenhoshou/nss-e.pdf.

46 Robert Ward, 'Japan's Security Policy and China', in *Asia-Pacific Regional Security Assessment 2021: Key Developments and Trends* (Abingdon: Routledge for the IISS, 2021), p. 34.

47 'Securing Japan: An Assessment of Japan's Strategy for Space', European Space Policy Institute, July 2020, p. 1, https://www.espi.or.at/wp-content/uploads/2022/06/ESPI-Report-74-Securing-Japan-Executive-Summary.pdf.

48 See 'Act on the Protection of Specially Designated Secrets', Japanese Law Translation, https://www.japaneselawtranslation.go.jp/en/laws/view/2543/en#:~:text=Article%2024(1)A%20person,act%20of%20unauthorized%20computer%20access.

49 Japan, Ministry of Defense, 'National Defense Program Guidelines for FY 2019 and Beyond', 18 December 2018, p. 20,

https://warp.da.ndl.go.jp/info:ndljp/pid/11591426/www.mod.go.jp/j/approach/agenda/guideline/2019/pdf/20181218_e.pdf. See also Yuka Koshino, 'Japan's New Space Domain Mission Unit and Security in the Indo-Pacific Region', IISS Military Balance Blog, 1 May 2020, https://www.iiss.org/online-analysis/military-balance/2020/05/japan-space-domain-mission-unit-security/.

50 Japan, Ministry of Foreign Affairs, 'The Guidelines for Japan–U.S. Defense Cooperation', 27 April 2015, https://www.mofa.go.jp/files/000078188.pdf, pp. 1, 21.

51 Japan, Cabinet Secretariat, 'National Security Strategy of Japan', December 2022, p. 23.

52 For a description of Japan's deployment of SIGINT during the incident of the Soviet Union's shooting down of a Korean Air airliner in 1983, see Brad Williams, *Japanese Foreign Intelligence and Grand Strategy: From the Cold War to the Abe Era* (Washington DC: Georgetown University Press, 2021), p. 1.

53 Yuka Koshino and Robert Ward, *Japan's Effectiveness as a Geo-economic Actor: Navigating Great-power Competition*, Adelphi 481–483 (Abingdon: Routledge for the IISS, 2022), pp. 53–4; and 'Cyber Capabilities and National Power: A Net Assessment', IISS, 28 June 2021, p. 79, https://www.iiss.org/globalassets/media-library---content--migration/files/research-papers/cyber-power-report/cyber-capabilities-and-national-power---a-net-assessment___.pdf.

54 For an illustration of some of the Japanese government's thinking on how to solve Japan's cyber-skills problems, see the comments of Okano Masataka, Deputy National Security Advisor, Cabinet Secretariat, Japan at the 2023 IISS Shangri-La Dialogue:

https://www.iiss.org/events/shangri-la-dialogue/shangri-la-dialogue-2023/special-sessions/.

55 'Japan's Defense Ministry to Set Up Cyber Department at Its Academy', *Nikkei Asia*, 10 January 2023, https://asia.nikkei.com/Politics/Japan-s-Defense-Ministry-to-set-up-cyber-department-at-its-academy#:~:text=The%20academy%20expects%20to%20begin,been%20working%20to%20strengthen%20cyberdefense. See also Japan, Ministry of Defense, 'Defense Buildup Program', 16 December 2022, https://www.mod.go.jp/j/policy/agenda/guideline/plan/pdf/program_en.pdf.

56 'Cyber Power – Tier Three', IISS, 28 June 2021, https://www.iiss.org/research-paper/2021/06/cyber-power---tier-three/.

57 Kotani Ken, 'Japan's Intelligence Capabilities', IISS Japan Memo podcast, 11 July 2024, https://www.iiss.org/podcasts/japan-memo/2024/07/japans-intelligence-capabilities-with-professor-richard-j-samuels-professor-kotani-ken-and-hosaka-sanshiro/. In addition to the Defense Intelligence Headquarters, these agencies are: the Cabinet Intelligence and Research Office (CIRO, in the Cabinet Secretariat), the Intelligence and Analysis Service and the International Counter-Terrorism Intelligence Collection Unit (IAS and CTU-J, both in the Ministry of Foreign Affairs), and the Public Security Intelligence Agency (PSIA, in the Ministry of Justice). See Kotani Ken, *Nihon Interigensu Shi, Kyū Nihon Gun Kara, Kōan, Naichō, NSC Made* [History of Japanese intelligence: from the former Japanese Army, public security, the Cabinet Intelligence and Research Office to the NSC] (Tokyo: Chuo Koron Shinsha, 2022), pp. ii–iv. This includes a chart showing how the

different intelligence organisations interact within the government hierarchy up to the prime minister.

58 Richard J. Samuels, *Special Duty: A History of the Japanese Intelligence Community* (Ithaca, NY: Cornell University Press, 2019).

59 Williams, *Japanese Foreign Intelligence and Grand Strategy: From the Cold War to the Abe Era*, p. 174.

60 Samuels, *Special Duty: A History of the Japanese Intelligence Community*.

61 'Cyber Capabilities and National Power: A Net Assessment', IISS, p. 82.

62 Samuels, *Special Duty: A History of the Japanese Intelligence Community*.

63 Kotani, *Nihon Interigensu Shi, Kyū Nihon Gun Kara, Kōan, Naichō, NSC Made*, p. 217.

64 'Japan's Intelligence Capabilities with Professor Richard J. Samuels, Professor Kotani Ken and Hosaka Sanshiro', IISS Japan Memo podcast, 11 July 2024, https://www.iiss.org/podcasts/japan-memo/2024/07/japans-intelligence-capabilities-with-professor-richard-j-samuels-professor-kotani-ken-and-hosaka-sanshiro/.

65 For example, Kono Taro, a former defence minister: see Daishi Abe and Rieko Miki, 'Japan Wants de Facto "Six Eyes" Intelligence Status: Defense Chief', *Nikkei Asia*, 14 August 2020, https://asia.nikkei.com/Editor-s-Picks/Interview/Japan-wants-de-facto-Six-Eyes-intelligence-status-defense-chief.

66 David Vergun, 'AUKUS Partners Consider Cooperation with Japan', US Department of Defense, 8 April 2024, https://www.defense.gov/News/News-Stories/Article/Article/3734336/aukus-partners-consider-cooperation-with-japan/.

67 Mari Yamaguchi, 'Japan, New Zealand Agree on Intel Sharing Pact amid Growing Regional Security Concerns', Associated Press,

19 June 2024, https://apnews.com/article/japan-new-zealand-security-9a74742d0c6e3441bf18c466c051daad.

68 Admiral Dong Jun's comments at the 2024 IISS Shangri-La Dialogue reflect this view. See Admiral Dong Jun, Minister of National Defense, China, 'China's Approach to Global Security', IISS Shangri-La Dialogue 2024, 2 June 2024, https://www.iiss.org/events/shangri-la-dialogue/shangri-la-dialogue-2024/plenary-sessions/fifth-plenary/.

69 'G7 Hiroshima Leaders' Communiqué', 20 May 2023, p. 36, https://www.consilium.europa.eu/media/64497/g7-2023-hiroshima-leaders-communiqu%C3%A9.pdf.

70 Gabriel Dominguez, 'Philippines Considering Trilateral Defense Pact with US and Japan', *Japan Times*, 13 February 2023, https://www.japantimes.co.jp/news/2023/02/13/national/philippines-tripartite-security-pact-us-japan/.

71 U.S.–China Economic and Security Review Commission, 'South China Sea Arbitration Ruling: What Happened and What's Next?', 12 July 2016, https://www.uscc.gov/sites/default/files/Research/Issue%20Brief_South%20China%20Sea%20Arbitration%20Ruling%20What%20Happened%20and%20What%27s%20Next071216.pdf.

72 Kardon, *China's Law of the Sea: The New Rules of Maritime Order*, p. 102.

73 Kelly Ng, 'What We Know About North Korean Troops Fighting Russia's War', BBC News, 24 December 2024, https://www.bbc.co.uk/news/articles/cm2796pdm1lo.

74 Jack Kim, 'Elite North Korea Military Trainees Visit Russia amid Deepening Ties', Reuters, 9 July 2024, https://www.reuters.com/world/elite-north-korea-military-trainees-visit-russia-amid-deepening-ties-2024-07-09/.

75 'The Spirit of Camp David: Joint Statement of Japan, the Republic of Korea, and the United States',

18 August 2023, https://www.mofa.
go.jp/files/100541826.pdf.

76 'The Nixon–Sato Communique',
New York Times, 22 November 1969,
https://timesmachine.nytimes.com/
timesmachine/1969/11/22/issue.html.

77 'The Spirit of Camp David: Joint
Statement of Japan, the Republic of
Korea, and the United States'.

78 Anthony Kuhn, 'U.S. Criticizes South
Korea After Seoul Scraps Intelligence-
sharing Pact with Tokyo', NPR,
30 August 2019, https://www.npr.
org/2019/08/30/755733522/u-s-criticizes-
south-korea-after-seoul-scraps-
intelligence-sharing-pact-with-tok.

79 Japan, Ministry of Foreign Affairs,
'Outcome of Prime Minister Kishida's
Attendance at the NATO Summit
Meeting, North Atlantic Treaty
Organization (NATO)', 29 June 2022,
https://www.nato.int/cps/en/natolive/
opinions_8019.htm. https://www.mofa.
go.jp/erp/ep/page4e_001264.html.

80 NATO, 'NATO Secretary General: No
Partner Is Closer than Japan', 12 July
2023, https://www.nato.int/cps/en/
natohq/news_217062.htm.

81 NATO, 'Japan and NATO: Toward
Further Collaboration', Statement
by Prime Minister Shinzo Abe to the
North Atlantic Council, 12 January
2007, https://www.nato.int/docu/
speech/2007/s070112b.html.

82 Japan, Ministry of Foreign Affairs,
'Prime Minister Shinzo Abe Meets
with the Secretary General of NATO',
6 July 2017, https://www.mofa.go.jp/
erp/ep/page1e_000165.html.

83 See, for example, NATO, 'NATO
2022 Strategic Concept', updated
3 March 2023, p. 5, https://www.
nato.int/nato_static_fl2014/assets/
pdf/2022/6/pdf/290622-strategic-
concept.pdf; and NATO, 'The North
Atlantic Treaty', 4 April 1949, https://
www.nato.int/cps/en/natohq/
official_texts_17120.htm.

Chapter Three

1 Japan, Cabinet Secretariat, 'National
Security Strategy of Japan', December
2022, p. 3, https://www.cas.go.jp/jp/
siryou/221216anzenhoshou/nss-e.pdf.

2 Dr Tobias Lindner, Minister of State
at the Federal Foreign Office of
Germany, 'Germany's First National
Security Strategy', IISS webinar,
22 June 2023, https://www.iiss.org/
events/2023/062/germanys-first-
national-security-strategy/, at about
50 minutes into the webinar.

3 Japan, Cabinet Secretariat, 'National
Security Strategy of Japan', p. 3.

4 For a list of Ohira's study groups,
see Seizaburo Satō, Ken'ichi Kōyama
and Shunpei Kumon, *Postwar
Politician: The Life of Former Prime
Minister Masayoshi Ōhira* (Tokyo and
New York: Kodansha International,

1990), p. 450. 'Nagatacho' is an area
in Tokyo also used as shorthand for
Japan's political community.

5 For a more detailed discussion of
Ohira's 'comprehensive security'
concept, see Yuka Koshino and
Robert Ward, *Japan's Effectiveness as a
Geo-economic Actor: Navigating Great-
power Competition, Adelphi* 481–483
(Abingdon: Routledge for the IISS,
2022), pp. 38–9.

6 See 'Sōgo Anzenhoshō Kenkyū
Gurūpu, Hōkokusho' [Report from
the Comprehensive Security Study
Group], 2 July 1980, The World
and Japan Database, Database of
Japanese Politics and International
Relations, National Graduate
Institute for Policy Studies (GRIPS),
Institute for Advanced Studies on

Asia (IASA), University of Tokyo, https://worldjpn.net/documents/texts/JPSC/19800702.O1J.html.

7   Tanaka Akihiko, *Anzen Hoshō, Sengo 50 Nen no Mosaku* [Security: an exploration 50 years after the end of the war] (Tokyo: Yomiuri Shimbunsha, 1997), p. 293.

8   Sakaiya Shiro, *Sengo Nihon Seiji Shi, Senryōki Kara 'Neo' 55 Taisei Made* [Post-war Japan's political history: from the occupation to the 'neo'-1955 system] (Tokyo: Chuo Koron Shinsha, 2023), p. 126.

9   'Sōgo Anzenhoshō Kenkyū Gurūpu, Hōkokusho' [Report from the Comprehensive Security Study Group]: '*Amerika keizai no chikara wa, zettaiteki ni mo, mata, Seiō shokoku to Nihon no keizai hatten ni yotte sōtaiteki ni mo, teika shita. Kono kekka, kokusai tsūka taisei ya jiyū bōeki taisei no iji wo jūrai to onaji yō ni Amerika ni ōkiku izon suru koto wa dekinaku natta.*' [US economic strength has declined absolutely and relatively as a result of the economic development of Western Europe countries and Japan. As a result, we can no longer rely on the US to support the international currency system and free trade.]

10 For an account of Deng's trip to Japan in 1978 and its impact on Sino-Japanese relations, see Ezra F. Vogel, *Deng Xiaoping and the Transformation of China* (Cambridge, MA: Belknap Press of Harvard University Press, 2011), pp. 297–310.

11 Sakaiya, *Sengo Nihon Seiji Shi, Senryōki Kara 'Neo' 55 Taisei Made* [Post-war Japan's political history: from the occupation to the 'neo'-1955 system], p. 103.

12 See, for example, Sato Taketsugu, 'Kōchikai no Senpai – Ōhira Masayoshi Shi ga Tonaeta "Sōgō Anpo" Ima Koso Sai Hyōka wo' [Now is the time to re-evaluate the 'comprehensive security' advocated by Ohira Masayoshi,

Kishida's Kochikai elder], *Asahi Shimbun*, 28 October 2022, https://www.asahi.com/articles/ASQBW6SQTQBVULZU00M.html.

13 'Japan's Intelligence Capabilities with Professor Richard J. Samuels, Professor Kotani Ken and Hosaka Sanshiro', IISS Japan Memo podcast, 11 July 2024, https://www.iiss.org/podcasts/japan-memo/2024/07/japans-intelligence-capabilities-with-professor-richard-j-samuels-professor-kotani-ken-and-hosaka-sanshiro/.

14 See, for example, Tsuyoshi Hasegawa, 'The Soviet Factor in U.S.–Japanese Defense Cooperation, 1978–1985', *Journal of Cold War Studies*, vol. 15, no. 2, Spring 2013, p. 80.

15 'Japan's Intelligence Capabilities with Professor Richard J. Samuels, Professor Kotani Ken and Hosaka Sanshiro'.

16 Douglas A. Irwin, 'The U.S.–Japan Semiconductor Trade Conflict', National Bureau of Economic Research, January 1996, p. 5, https://www.nber.org/system/files/chapters/c8717/c8717.pdf.

17 George P. Shultz, *Turmoil and Triumph: My Years as Secretary of State* (New York: Scribner, 1993), p. 243.

18 Walter LaFeber, *The Clash: U.S.–Japanese Relations Throughout History* (New York: W. W. Norton & Company, 1997), p. 392.

19 Glenn D. Hook et al., *Japan's International Relations: Politics, Economics and Security*, 2nd ed. (London: Routledge, 2005), p. 230.

20 For a discussion of geo-economic power and how it relates to Japan, see Koshino and Ward, *Japan's Effectiveness as a Geo-economic Actor: Navigating Great-power Competition*, pp. 1–16.

21 See *Ibid.*, pp. 76–7, for a fuller discussion of the APEC headwinds in the 1990s.

22 'Clinton's Words on China: Trade
Is the Smart Thing', *New York Times*,
9 March 2000, https://www.nytimes.
com/2000/03/09/world/clinton-s-words-
on-china-trade-is-the-smart-thing.html.

23 For the government's view of the
desired impact of the 'Abenomics'
economic programme, see Japan, Prime
Minister's Office, 'The Three Arrows
of "Abenomics" – Growth Strategy/the
Third Arrow as a Key to Achieve the
Revitalization of Japan', https://japan.
kantei.go.jp/letters/message/abenomics/
TheThreeArrowsOfAbenomics_EN.pdf.

24 See, for example, Abe Shinzo,
Utsukushii Kuni E [Towards a
beautiful country] (Tokyo: Bunshun
Shinsho, 2006), p. 129.

25 Japan, Ministry of Foreign Affairs,
'The 13th IISS Asian Security
Summit – The Shangri-La Dialogue:
Keynote Address by Shinzo Abe,
Prime Minister of Japan', 30 May
2014, https://www.mofa.go.jp/fp/nsp/
page4e_000086.html.

26 For a list of Japanese sanctions
against Russia to date, see, for
example, 'Japanese Imposed
Sanctions', Baker McKenzie Global
Sanctions and Export Controls
blog, https://sanctionsnews.
bakermckenzie.com/category/
sanctions-regimes/other-sanctions/
japanese-imposed-sanctions/.

27 Jaroslav Lukiv and Jean Mackenzie,
'G7 Agrees $50bn Loan for Ukraine
from Russian Assets', BBC News, 13
June 2024, https://www.bbc.co.uk/
news/articles/cllldqyg19ro.

28 Osamu Nariai, *History of the Modern
Japanese Economy* (Tokyo: Foreign
Press Center Japan, 1999), pp. 48–9.

29 Mireya Solis, *Japan's Quiet Leadership:
Reshaping the Indo-Pacific* (Washington
DC: Brookings Institution Press,
2023), p. 201.

30 Japan, Ministry of Finance, 'Rules and
Regulations of the Foreign Exchange
and Foreign Trade Act', 24 April 2020,
p. 2, https://www.mof.go.jp/english/

policy/international_policy/fdi/
kanrenshiryou01_20200424.pdf.

31 For more details on the Economic
Security Promotion Act, see 'Japan's
Economic Security Promotion Act
and the Implications for Business',
IISS *Strategic Comments*, vol. 28, no.
32, 9 December 2022, https://www.
iiss.org/publications/strategic-
comments/2022/japans-economic-
security-promotion-act-and-the-
implications-for-businesses/.

32 For an excellent account of the
intricacies of Japan's security-
clearance regulatory architecture, see
Hirohito Ogi, 'Remaining Challenges
for Operationalizing Japan's
Information Security Legislation',
AP Initiative, 22 March 2024, https://
apinitiative.org/en/2024/03/22/56813/.

33 Chalmers Johnson, *MITI and the
Japanese Miracle: The Growth of
Industrial Policy, 1925–1975* (Stanford,
CA: Stanford University Press, 1982).

34 The terms 'strategic autonomy'
and 'strategic indispensability'
are associated with proposals put
forward in 2020–21 by the LDP's
Policy Research Council. See, for
example, 'The Urgent Need to
Establish "Strategic Autonomy"
and "Strategic Indispensability"
– Economic Security Strategy for
a Digital Transformation Society',
13 October 2021, https://www.
japanpolicyforum.jp/diplomacy/
pt2021101308092511642.html. See
also Kazuto Suzuki, 'The Shift from
Economic Security to Geoeconomics',
Institute of Geoeconomics, 17 April
2024, https://instituteofgeoeconomics.
org/en/research/2024041757188/.

35 'TSMC no Dai 2 Kōjō Kensetsu,
Nihon ni Donna Eikyō?' [What
will be the impact on Japan of
TSMC's second factory?], *Nihon
Keizai Shimbun*, 7 February 2024,
https://www.nikkei.com/article/
DGXZQODL069900W4A200C
2000000/.

36   See 'Japan's Economic-security Policy with Professor Suzuki Kazuto and Dr Elli-Katharina Pohlkamp', IISS Japan Memo podcast, 13 February 2025, https://www.iiss.org/podcasts/japan-memo/2025/02/japans-economic-security-policy-with-professor-suzuki-kazuto-and-dr-elli-katharina-pohlkamp/.

37   Riho Nagao, 'TSMC Plans to Produce 6-nm Chips in 2nd Japan Plant', *Nikkei Asia*, 12 October 2023, https://asia.nikkei.com/Business/Tech/Semiconductors/TSMC-plans-to-produce-6-nm-chips-in-2nd-Japan-plant; and 'TSMC Confirms Kikuyo as Site for 2nd Japanese Fab', Focus Taiwan, 7 April 2024, https://focustaiwan.tw/business/202404070004.

38   'TSMC Opens 1st Japan Chip Plant amid Supply Chain Concerns', Kyodo News, 24 February 2024, https://english.kyodonews.net/news/2024/02/dff151183ed0-tsmc-opens-1st-japan-chip-factory-more-investment-planned.html.

39   'TSMC Kōjō Kansei, Kawaru Kumamoto, Shirikon Airando Saikō E' [TSMC factory completed: changing Kumamoto, reviving Silicon Island], *Nihon Keizai Shimbun*, 2 February 2022, https://www.nikkei.com/telling/DGXZTS00009090X00C24A2000000/; and Riho Nagao, 'TSMC Plans to Produce 6-nm Chips in 2nd Japan Plant'.

40   Morikita Kikuma and Sugiura Nami, 'TSMC ga Yatte Kita, Kumamoto de Susumu Kokusaika, Chika Kōtō ni Tsuzuku Hakyū mo' [TSMC has arrived in Kumamoto: internationalisation is progressing, with repercussions following rising land prices], *Asahi Shimbun*, 22 February 2024, https://www.asahi.com/articles/ASS2N6R90S2NTLVB007.html.

41   Wataru Suzuki, 'Toyota to Invest in TSMC Arm for 2nd Kumamoto Chip Plant in Japan', *Nikkei Asia*, 6 February 2024, https://asia.nikkei.com/Business/Business-deals/Toyota-to-invest-in-TSMC-arm-for-2nd-Kumamoto-chip-plant-in-Japan.

42   Nagahashi Akifumi and Tanaka Kanako, 'Keisansho, Rapidasu Tsuika Shien, Jisedai Handōtai, Saidai 5900 Oku En' [METI to provide additional support to Rapidus for next-generation semiconductors, up to ¥590 billion], *Asahi Shimbun*, 2 April 2024, https://www.asahi.com/articles/DA3S15903023.html?iref=ogimage_rek.

43   Ryohtaroh Satoh, 'Rapidus: How a Phone Call from IBM Reignited Japan's Chip Ambitions', *Nikkei Asia*, 2 August 2024, https://asia.nikkei.com/Business/Business-Spotlight/Rapidus-How-a-phone-call-from-IBM-reignited-Japan-s-chip-ambitions.

44   Mukaino Ryo, Okada Tatsuya and Nagao Riho, 'Rapidasu Tōi Ryōsan, 4 Chō En Fusoku Handōtai Saikō e Sei-Kan-Min Danketsu wo' [Rapidus is far from mass production, ¥4 trillion shortfall; government, bureaucracy and the private sector must unite to revive the semiconductor sector], *Nihon Keizai Shimbun*, 10 September 2024, https://www.nikkei.com/article/DGXZQOUC290QP0Z20C24A8000000/.

45   Robin Kwong, 'Elpida Files for Bankruptcy Protection', *Financial Times*, 27 February 2012, https://www.ft.com/content/db64c462-6127-11e1-8a8e-00144feabdc0.

Chapter Four

1   Colin S. Gray, *The Geopolitics of Super Power* (Lexington, KY: The University Press of Kentucky, 1988), p. 15.

2   Jakub Grygiel, 'Educating for National Security', *Orbis*, vol. 57, no. 2, Spring 2013, pp. 201–16.

3   George P. Shultz, *Turmoil and Triumph: My Years as Secretary of State* (New York: Scribner, 1993), p. 244.

4   Iskander Rehman, *Planning for Protraction: A Historically Informed Approach to Great-power War and Sino-US Competition*, Adelphi 496–497 (Abingdon: Routledge for the IISS, 2023), p. 19.

5   Bill Emmott, *Deterrence, Diplomacy and the Risk of Conflict over Taiwan*, Adelphi 508–510 (Abingdon: Routledge for the IISS, 2024), pp. 56–8.

6   See Christopher W. Hughes, *Japan as a Global Military Power: New Capabilities, Alliance Integration, Bilateralism-plus* (Cambridge: Cambridge University Press, 2022), pp. 1–2, for an outline of the inventory of Japan's armed forces.

7   World Bank, 'GDP (current US$) – China, Japan', https://data.worldbank.org/indicator/NY.GDP.MKTP.CD?locations=CN-JP.

8   *Ibid.*

9   Yuka Koshino and Robert Ward, *Japan's Effectiveness as a Geo-economic Actor: Navigating Great-power Competition*, Adelphi 481–483 (Abingdon: Routledge for the IISS, 2022), p. 15.

10 Japan, Ministry of Defense, 'Defense Buildup Program', 16 December 2022, p. 4, https://www.mod.go.jp/j/policy/agenda/guideline/plan/pdf/program_en.pdf.

11 See Yasuaki Chijiwa, 'Unfinished "Beyond-the-threat Theory" – Japan's "Basic Defense Force Concept" Revisited', *NIDS Journal of Defense and Security*, 17 December 2016, pp. 83–5, https://www.nids.mod.go.jp/english/publication/kiyo/pdf/2016/bulletin_e2016_6.pdf.

12 Mark Fitzpatrick, *Asia's Latent Nuclear Powers: Japan, South Korea and Taiwan*, Adelphi 455 (Abingdon: Routledge for the IISS, 2016), pp. 98–9.

13 See, for example, the comments of veteran politician Ozawa Ichiro: Jonathan Watts, 'Japan "Could Build 7,000 Nuclear Bombs"', *Guardian*, 8 April 2002, https://www.theguardian.com/world/2002/apr/08/japan.jonathanwatts. After the 2011 Fukushima nuclear disaster, Ishiba Shigeru, defense minister at the time and at this writing prime minister, argued that Japan should keep the nuclear fuel cycle to maintain 'technical deterrence'. See Fitzpatrick, *Asia's Latent Nuclear Powers: Japan, South Korea and Taiwan*, p. 81.

14 Jesse Johnson, 'Japan Should Consider Hosting U.S. Nuclear Weapons, Abe Says', *Japan Times*, 27 February 2022, https://www.japantimes.co.jp/news/2022/02/27/national/politics-diplomacy/shinzo-abe-japan-nuclear-weapons-taiwan/.

15 Kishida Fumio, 'Keynote Address', 19th Regional Security Summit, The Shangri-La Dialogue, 10 June 2022, https://www.iiss.org/globalassets/media-library---content--migration/files/shangri-la-dialogue/2022/transcripts/keynote-address/kishida-fumio-prime-minister-japan-as-delivered.pdf.

16 'What If South Korea Got a Nuclear Bomb?', *The Economist*, 15 August 2024, https://www.economist.com/asia/2024/08/15/what-if-south-korea-got-a-nuclear-bomb.

17 Initially, Sato had only intended two non-nuclear principles: that Japan would not possess or produce nuclear weapons. But this was not felt to be strong enough by the LDP's Committee on General Affairs. Sato's non-nuclear policy was also connected to the discussions with the US on the reversion of Okinawa to Japanese control and Japanese concerns about nuclear weapons being hosted on US bases in Okinawa after reversion. The non-nuclear principles and Okinawa reversion negotiations should also be seen within the context of the then-looming extension in 1970 of the US–Japan security treaty. Sato was keen to avoid the large-scale anti-treaty demonstrations that had ultimately brought Kishi's government down in 1960. See Tanaka Akihiko, *Anzen Hoshō, Sengo 50 Nen no Mosaku* [Security: an exploration 50 years after the end of the war] (Tokyo: Yomiuri Shimbunsha, 1997), pp. 215–25, for a discussion of Japan's threat perceptions at the time and the link with the Okinawa reversion negotiations.

18 Farah Master, 'China's Population Drops for Second Year, with Record Low Birth Rate', Reuters, 17 January 2024, https://www.reuters.com/world/china/chinas-population-drops-2nd-year-raises-long-term-growth-concerns-2024-01-17/.

19 'Can the Rich World Escape Its Baby Crisis?', *The Economist*, 21 May 2024, https://www.economist.com/finance-and-economics/2024/05/21/can-the-rich-world-escape-its-baby-crisis.

20 Chiba Takurō and Meguro Takayuki, 'Jinkō Gen, Zen Todōfuken de, Saita 80 Man Nin Gen, 1 Gatsu Jiten' [Population decline in all prefectures, the largest ever decline of 800,000 people as of January], *Asahi Shimbun*, 26 July 2023, https://www.asahi.com/articles/DA3S15699882.html.

21 Chiba Takurō, 'Jinkō 86 Man Nin Gen, Saidaihaba, Gaikokujin, Hatsu no 300 Man Nin Chō' [Population falls by 860,000, the largest drop in the country's population; foreigners exceed 3 million for the first time], *Asahi Shimbun*, 25 July 2024, https://www.asahi.com/articles/DA3S15993077.html.

22 Tominaga Shinnojyō , 'Jieitai, Mamori no Jūshin wo Nishi ni, 10 Nen de Okinawa no Shisetsu wa 4 Wari zō' [Self-Defense Forces shift centre of defence to the west, facilities in Okinawa increase by 40% in 10 years], *Nihon Keizai Shimbun*, 2 July 2024, https://www.nikkei.com/article/DGXZQOUA2417T0U4A620C2000000/.

23 *Ibid*.

24 Richard J. Samuels, *3.11: Disaster and Change in Japan* (Ithaca, NY and London: Cornell University Press, 2013).

25 'Jieikan no Saiyō Ritsu 50.8%, Kako Saitei' [Self-Defense Force recruitment rate hits record low of 50.8%], *Asahi Shimbun*, 8 July 2024, https://www.asahi.com/articles/DA3S15977845.html.

26 For a discussion on Japan's difficulties in recruiting for submarines, see Veerle Nouwens and Ken Moriyasu, 'Episode 20: Japan's Security in 2021: A New Defence White Paper', Bridging the Oceans Podcast, RUSI, 21 July 2021, https://rusi.org/podcasts/bridging-the-oceans/episode-20-japans-security-2021-new-defence-white-paper (around 19.40 minutes into the podcast).

27 Dzirhan Mahadzir, 'Japan Ministry of Defense Unveils Record High FY2025 Budget Request', NSNI News, 4 September 2024, https://news.usni.org/2024/09/04/japan-ministry-of-defense-unveils-record-high-fy-2025-budget-request.

28 '"Defure Jidai" Hikizuru Bōchō Yosan, 25 Nendo Yōkyū 117 Chō

En Chō' [Inflated budget hangover from the deflation era: request for over ¥117 trillion in fiscal year 2025], *Nihon Keizai Shimbun*, 31 August 2024, https://www.nikkei.com/ article/DGXZQOUA302MK0 Q4A830C2000000/.

29   Tanaka, *Anzen Hoshō, Sengo 50 Nen no Mosaku* [Security: an exploration 50 years after the end of the war], p. 301.

30   NATO, 'Defence Expenditures and NATO's 2% Guideline', 18 June 2024, https://www.nato.int/cps/en/natohq/ topics_49198.htm.

31   IMF, 'General Government Gross Debt', https://www. imf.org/external/datamapper/ GGXWDG_NGDP@WEO/ JPN?zoom=JPN&highlight=JPN.

32   *Ibid.*, https://www.imf. org/external/datamapper/ GGXWDG_NGDP@WEO/ ITA?zoom=ITA&highlight=ITA.

33   *Ibid.*, https://www.imf.org/external/ datamapper/GGXWDN_G01_ GDP_PT@FM/ADVEC/FM_EMG/ FM_LIDC/JPN.

34   Japan, Ministry of Finance, 'Japanese Government Bonds, August 2024 Newsletter', p. 15, https://www. mof.go.jp/english/policy/jgbs/ publication/newsletter/jgb2024_ 08e.pdf.

35   OECD, 'Revenue Statistics 2024 – Japan', https://www.oecd.org/ content/dam/oecd/en/topics/policy- sub-issues/global-tax-revenues/ revenue-statistics-japan.pdf.

36   Japan, Ministry of Finance, Draft Budgets for Fiscal Years 2024–25, 2010–11 and 2000–01. See, respectively, https://www.mof. go.jp/english/policy/budget/budget/ fy2024/01.pdf, https://warp.da.ndl. go.jp/info:ndljp/pid/11424711/ www.mof.go.jp/english/budget/ budget/fy2010/e20091225a.pdf, and https://warp.da.ndl.go.jp/info:ndljp/ pid/11424711/www.mof.go.jp/

english/budget/budget/fy2000/ e1b056.pdf.

37   The first socialist prime minister was Katayama Tetsu in 1947–48 and the second was Murayama Tomiichi in 1994–96.

38   John Dower writes of how, as a result of US-led post-war education reform, the Ministry of Education switched from being 'a vigilant watchdog of emperor-system ultranationalism' to 'one of the country's most systematic and zealous proponents of "peace and democracy"'. See John Dower, *Embracing Defeat: Japan and the Aftermath of World War II* (London: Penguin Books, 1999), pp. 246–51, for an account of post-war education reform.

39   Science Council of Japan, 'Statement on Research for Military Security', 24 March 2017, p. 1, https://www.scj. go.jp/ja/info/kohyo/pdf/kohyo-23- s243-en.pdf.

40   Koshino and Ward, *Japan's Effectiveness as a Geo-Economic Actor: Navigating Great-power Competition*, pp. 113–14.

41   Kentaro Tsutsumi and Mayumi Kuze, 'Mitsubishi Heavy Leads Japan's Defense-sector Rally as Market Roils', *Nikkei Asia*, 10 August 2024, https://asia. nikkei.com/Business/Markets/ Equities/Mitsubishi-Heavy-leads- Japan-s-defense-sector-rally-as- market-roils#:~:text=Higher%20 profitability%20is%20 providing%20a,profitable%20 orders%20in%20its%20portfolio.

42   Koshino and Ward, *Japan's Effectiveness as a Geo-Economic Actor: Navigating Great-power Competition*, p. 27.

43   Japan, Cabinet Secretariat, 'National Security Strategy of Japan', December 2022, p. 12, https://www.cas.go.jp/jp/ siryou/221216anzenhoshou/ nss-e.pdf.

44 *Ibid.*, pp. 12, 21.

45 *Ibid.*, p. 21.

46 In this *Nikkei* survey conducted immediately after the publication of the new national-security documents, over 50% of those surveyed supported the strengthening of Japan's defence capabilities. See 'Zōzei Setsumei "Fujūbun" 84%, Jiki Kettei Sakiokuri "Futekisetsu" 50%' [84% say explanation for tax increase is 'inadequate'; 50% say postponement of decision on tax increase is 'inappropriate'], *Nihon Keizai Shimbun*, 26 December 2022, https://www.nikkei.com/article/DGXZQOUA22D5S0S2A221C2000000/.

47 '84% of People Nationwide Say They Feel Japan's National Security Is Under Threat', *Japan News by the Yomiuri Shimbun*, 8 April 2024, https://japannews.yomiuri.co.jp/politics/defense-security/20240408-179132/.

48 '92.1% in Japan View China Unfavourably, Says Japan–China Public Opinion Survey', *Japan News by the Yomiuri Shimbun*, 11 October 2023, https://japannews.yomiuri.co.jp/politics/politics-government/20231011-142389/.

49 The trajectory of the Japan Socialist Party (JSP) is emblematic of this. At its most recent peak, in the 1990 lower-house election, the party won around 25% of the seats. A combination of the impact of the political realignment in Japan since the mid-1990s and changes in the international environment (including the collapse of the Soviet Union) meant its support fell after this. In the 2009 general election, for example, in which the LDP was ejected from power for the first time since 1993, the JSP's successor party, the Social Democratic Party, won only 5% of the vote. In the 2021 general election the JSP won one seat.

50 Colin S. Gray, 'National Style in Strategy: The American Example', *International Security*, vol. 6, no. 2, Fall 1981, pp. 24–5.

51 *Ibid.*, p. 21.

52 For a more detailed discussion of Kosaka's 'maritime nation' vs 'island nation' thesis, see Koshino and Ward, *Japan's Effectiveness as a Geo-Economic Actor: Navigating Great-power Competition*, pp. 103–4.

53 Roger Boyes, 'Chinese Threat Calls for Five Eyes Expansion', *The Times*, 16 November 2021, https://www.thetimes.com/world/us-world/article/chinese-threat-calls-for-five-eyes-expansion-bkkxwh8rv.

54 Coral Bell, *The Asian Balance of Power: A Comparison with European Precedents*, *Adelphi Papers*, no. 44 (London: IISS, 1968), pp. 2–3.

55 Robert Ward et al., 'The Japan–UK Strategic Partnership and Europe's Engagement in the Indo-Pacific', IISS Japan Chair webinar, 3 October 2023, https://www.iiss.org/events/2023/10/the-japan-uk-strategic-partnership-and-europes-engagement-in-the-indo-pacific/ (about 1 hour 79 minutes).

56 Michael Howard, 'Grand Strategy in the Twentieth Century', *Defence Studies*, vol.1, no. 1, Spring 2001, p. 2.

Conclusion

1   Bernard Brodie, quoted in Zachary Jonathan Jacobson, *On Nixon's Madness: An Emotional History* (Baltimore, MD: Johns Hopkins University Press, 2023), p. 219.

2   For Hatoyama's thinking behind his East Asian Community idea, see Japan, Prime Minister's Office, 'Address by H.E. Dr. Yukio Hatoyama Prime Minister of Japan, Japan's New Commitment to Asia, Toward the Realization of an East Asian Community', 15 November 2009, https://japan.kantei.go.jp/hatoyama/statement/200911/15singapore_e.html.

3   Koga Daiki, 'Ji Kō to mo Saishō, Rikken wa Yokobai, Shūinsen Hirei Hyō' [Proportional representation votes in the House of Representatives election: both the LDP and Komeito have the lowest vote shares, while the Constitutional Democratic Party remains stable], *Asahi Shimbun*, 2 November 2024, https://www.asahi.com/articles/DA3S16074446.html.

4   'Fewer People Are Willing to Fight for Their Country Compared to Ten Years Ago', Gallup International, 25 March 2024, https://gallup-international.com/survey-results-and-news/survey-result/fewer-people-are-willing-to-fight-for-their-country-compared-to-ten-years-ago.

5   Matthew Smith, 'More Than a Third of Under-40s Would Refuse Conscription in the Event of a World War', YouGov, 26 January 2024, https://yougov.co.uk/politics/articles/48473-more-than-a-third-of-under-40s-would-refuse-conscription-in-the-event-of-a-world-war.

6   'Poll: 63% Support Constitutional Revision Amid Japan's Changing Security Environment; 93% Cite National Security Risk from China', *Japan News by the Yomiuri Shimbun*, 3 May 2024, https://japannews.yomiuri.co.jp/politics/politics-government/20240503-183778/.

7   John Keegan, *The Second World War* (London: PIMLICO, 1989), p. 306.

INDEX

Note: Page numbers are italicised where terms appear in figures or maps.